MAN'S INGORANCE AND GOD'S GRACE

A Case For Conditional Immortality

Roger Galstad, PhD.

Serene,

Thank you for your faithfulness and wonderful example. May God richly bless you.

Roger

MAN'S INGORANCE AND GOD'S GRACE

A CASE FOR CONDITIONAL IMMORTALITY

© 2012 by Roger Galstad, PhD.

All rights reserved. No part of this book may be reproduced or transmitted in any form, or by any method, electronic or mechanical, without written permission of the author.

First Printing
ISBN: 978-1-937064-15-0

**Printed in the USA by Trinity Press Publishing, LLC
Newburgh, Indiana 47630**
+

Dedication

To my lovely wife June, because of your patience in putting up with mounds of books and constant disarray in my office for the last two years. More important, you are the one person in the whole world with whom I could share my most intimate thoughts regarding matters of the afterlife, the nature of the soul, and errant traditional teachings refuted in this book. May God bless you richly and eternally for your saintly example.

Acknowledgements

I want to give credit where credit is due in acknowledging those who have contributed their thoughts regarding this book from the time of its inception through its completion. My friend, Nevin Nolder, has offered his mature perspective, guidance and appreciation for the basic thesis of this volume. Dr. Michael Lindsay, Professor Emeritus, UW, Eau Claire, WI, for his interest and encouragement regarding the process of the development of this thesis. The Reverend Emil W. Evenson, MDiv., ELCA retired, for his active interest and encouragement regarding the project. Especially helpful was his recalling his own seminary days when his professor encouraged him and his fellow seminarians to incorporate these ideas into their own ministries. Trinity Theological Seminary Professor Dr. Rick Fairman, PhD, my first reader, for his patient endurance with me through the Dissertation process and his encouragement regarding its publication. Dr. Ray L. Parker, PhD, for his kind, enthusiastic and helpful encouragement when this book was in the Dissertation stage and for his giving me the opportunity for the publication of this volume through Trinity Press. Finally, I am filled with gratitude for the constant support and encouragement of my congregation including the fact that they have been willing guinea pigs in my teaching them the scriptural views and principles expressed in these pages.

My sincerest gratitude to all of you.

TABLE OF CONTENTS
Chapter

One: Introduction 2

Two: Man's Ignorance 7
    I. Paul's Statement At Mar's Hill 9
    II. Father Forgive Them For They Know Not What They Do 19
    III. If You Were Blind You Would Have No Sin 25

Three: Man's Mortality 31
    I. The Origin Of The Soul In Scripture 31
    II. Hebrew And Greek Terms For Soul 36
    III. Only God Is Immortal 48
    IV. Plato 49
    V. Augustine 51
    VI. Paul On The State Of The Dead 55

Four: Annihilationism In Scripture 61
    I. The Lord Our God Is A Consuming Fire 61
    II. The Lake Of Fire As The Second Death 65
    III. The Wicked Become Ashes 66
    IV. Full Knowledge Of Salvation Will Be Given To All ... 70

Five: The Old Testament View Of Death 75
    I. Sheol 75
    II. Spirit, Body And Soul 77
    III. Enoch 80
    IV. Elijah 83
    V. Three Heavens 84
    VI. Heaven's Postal Service 85
    VII. Phillip 87
    VIII. Job 88

	IX.	Daniel and the Judgement	89
	X.	Resurrection in the Old Testament	92
	XI.	Ezekiel's Valley Of Dry Bones	93
	XII.	Pharisaic Concept Of Death	96

Six: The New Testament View Of Death 100
    I.   Jesus' Teaching On The State Of The Dead 101
    II.   Jairus' Daughter 104
    III. Jesus And The Thief On The Cross 107
    IV. Paul At Home With The Lord 110
    V.   Lazarus And The Rich Man 112
    VI. The Reformers 116
    VII. John Wycliffe 116
    VIII. Martin Luther 117
    IX. John Calvin 122
    X.   William Tyndale 124

Seven: Ever Burning And Ever Suffering In Hell Fire? 129
    I.   Traditional Orthodox Position 133
    II.   Unquenchable Fire 136
    III. Fudge's View 140
    IV. Luther 142

Eight: God's Grace 148
    I.   God Does Not Punish For Ignorance 148
    II.   God's Grace Must Be Taught 150
    III. God's Enemies Will Be Converted 155

Nine: Conclusion 162

Bibliography 166

CHAPTER ONE

INTRODUCTION

Chapter One

Introduction

*I commend thy soul to God the Father Almighty,
and thy body to the ground, earth to earth, ashes to ashes,
dust to dust, in sure and certain hope of resurrection to eternal life,
through our Lord Jesus Christ, who shall change our vile body,
that it may be like to his glorious body, according to the mighty working
whereby he is able to subdue all things to himself.*[1]

My grandfather, Olaf Wivelstad, died when I was ten years old. He had been an important part of my early life in providing a quiet strength and companionship. In the First World War he had survived a gas attack and a subsequent bayonet charge by the Germans and had been left for dead on the battlefield.

I remember staying overnights with my grandparents and hearing him cough seemingly interminably each morning before he could get out of bed. This was the result of his war wounds in addition to smoking a pack or two of Camels each day.

It was just after Memorial Day weekend, 1960, when we received word that grandpa had died of a heart attack. During the funeral, it was easily perceived by this ten year old grandson that the pastor conducting the funeral did not believe my grandfather was in heaven. By his attitude I sensed that he believed that my grandfather was actually in hell. My grandfather had not been known for his church going and rarely darkened the doorstep of a house of worship except for the inherent familial obligations of his attendance at weddings, funerals, baptisms and confirmations. Other than those occasions I never knew him to attend a church service.

For the first time in my life grandpa's funeral had brought me face to face with the possibility of an eternity in excruciating hell fire. Radio and television preachers had made me aware that there was a hell that is reserved for evil unbelievers. Facing that possibility has given me a particular interest in the matter of salvation, and on the other hand, eternal punishment. That interest has resulted in this book.

My formative years included an increasing awareness of God, the Bible,

---

[1] *J. Parker, editor, The First Prayer-Book...of King Edward VI [1549], (Oxford and London, 1883), 79 (This official committal prayer pointed to a growing acceptance of the reformation psychopannychist view that it is on resurrection day that the promises of Scripture regarding eternal life for the believer will be fulfilled.)*

theology and a variety of doctrinal positions by various churches. It became evident that most churches adopted conventional traditional Christian teaching on heaven and hell, the immortality of the soul and a host of other issues. But with time, study and experience, it became apparent that there were alternative views to those offered by mainline churches. Consequently, it is my purpose in this work to add substantially to the available knowledge regarding biblical salvation by reexamining our traditional theology. The purpose of this work is to make a strong selective biblical case for Conditional Immortality. Conditional Immortality is the position that recognizes that the human soul is not immortal at this moment. In this life it is quite mortal. The Bible reveals that believers will be granted immortality at the second coming and not before. Scripture also demonstrates that God, in his mercy, makes adequate provision for salvation opportunity for all humanity either in this life or at the time of judgment after the second resurrection.

Revulsion at the prospect of eternal agony in hell has caused me to see the Bible in a whole new light. This book is an attempt to document the discoveries from Scripture and the writings of a few theologians pertaining to the matter of the eternal destiny of man. Certainly this document is contrary to popular teaching and it will be troubling to those who are unfamiliar with the minority position in Christianity called Conditional Immortality.[2] Nevertheless, the position needs to be stated.

Clarity will be brought to the matter of salvation and its depth of acceptance. This work will take issue with traditional Christian teaching with a resolve to make a significant contribution to the theological-doctrinal positions that touch upon the matter of Conditional Immortality.

Chapter two presents a biblical statement, which seems to be overlooked in mainstream Christian Theology. That statement by Paul is:

> Acts 17:30 Therefore having overlooked the times of ignorance, God is now declaring to men that all people everywhere should repent.

In all the Bible study, attendance of church services, attending seminary courses and reading authors of Christian books, never in my life until recently, has this Scripture and its vital import ever come to light. That statement by Paul reveals the magnificent character of our God in that he overlooks our ignorance. The implications of that statement, and others discussed in chapter two, cannot help but cause us to reconsider our view of the judgment of God. Demonstration will be made that, according to

---

[2] *Bryan W. Ball, The Soul Sleepers, Christian Mortalism from Wycliffe to Priestley. (Cambridge, James Clarke & Co., 2008), 22.*

Scripture, God does not hold us accountable for what we do not understand. This fact alone ought to give us considerable pause as to how we see the judgment and salvation.

Chapter three plays an important part in the consideration of the state of the dead and the purpose of God for man. Conditional Immortality considers the mortality of the soul in order to determine how and when eternal life begins. These matters are intimately related. The mortality or immortality of the soul must be evaluated in developing a theology regarding eternal life and the most troublesome questions pertaining to the life, death and the condition of the soul. With a biblical perspective on this issue a large portion of traditional Christian theology is brought into question.

Another important consideration regarding salvation and the possibility of conditional or near universal salvation is the matter of the punishment of the wicked. Do the wicked continue consciously forever in an eternal state of agonizing pain and suffering or is their punishment of relatively short duration? The possibility of annihilation for the wicked will be dealt with in chapter four and will support my position as well as demonstrating the genuine loving grace and mercy of God expressed even to those who hate him.

Chapter five explores death as seen in the record of Old Testament Scripture. The Hebrew perspective on *sheol* and on the resurrection will be dealt with. The question must be answered regarding whether life continues after physical death, in heaven or hell or whether there is a temporary hiatus of life between death and the resurrection in what Jesus referred to as "sleep." Chapter five explains the import of the apparent transportation of Enoch and Elijah to heaven, both from a biblical and also from a secular historical standpoint.

Death and the resurrection are examined from the New Testament perspective in chapter six. This chapter will explain the position of Scripture and how it opposes the doctrines of traditional Christianity in regards to both limited and universal salvation. The chapter deals with whether the realized immortality of believers begins at physical death or at the resurrection of believers at the eschaton. The question is asked and explored as to whether believers are alive in heaven, asleep in the grave, or in some shadowy intermediate state.

If God is so merciful as to overlook our ignorance and that his purpose and desire are for our salvation, is he also merciful to those who ultimately may reject him? This question is developed and answered in chapter seven. Various theological views will be explored as to which best fits a conditionalist perspective.

Chapter eight deals with the matter of God's grace. He desires that all people be saved and he shows mercy on all in the achievement of that goal. Though not all men will subjectively accept his offer of grace, certainly most people will accept it and that will be included in the subject matter of chapter eight.

The Conclusion of this work, in chapter nine, will include drawing the salient points from each chapter into a cogent presentation of the supporting evidence of Scripture, theologians, and the sovereign perseverance of the Holy Spirit in the salvation of virtually all mankind.

Chapter Two
Man's Ignorance

CHAPTER TWO

MAN'S IGNORANCE

*I have many more things to say to you
but you cannot bear them now.*
John 16:12

*We don't want to rock our theological boat for fear of capsizing
And drowning in a sea of doctrinal relativism and spiritual confusion.
So we hold tightly to our conveniently held beliefs,
even if they don't make sense.*[3]

Since the day of Adam's creation, in the Garden of Eden, to our present day and on into eternity, mankind has been, is, and always will be ignorant of the absolute fullness of the mind and nature of God. Beginning at Eden, the Lord has revealed himself only slowly over time in small bits and pieces in his slow but careful and methodical unveiling of himself and his plan for mankind as we have become able to bear it.

Man has asked, at various times and in sundry ways, the question that resounded in the ears of Jesus and his disciples on the day of his triumphal entry into Jerusalem. "Who is this (Matthew 21:10)?" It seems that many people both of Jesus' day and ours, have in most cases, heard of Jesus but very few really seem to know, with any depth of understanding, just who he is and what is really required of us for salvation. On the whole, it seems evident that mankind is ignorant as to the person of our salvation. Jesus, as our redemptive Savior, has not been fully declared and proclaimed to every last soul who has ever lived. Consequently much of humanity has not been exposed to the saving knowledge of Jesus Christ in the manner and degree that is necessary for full accountability and commitment to him. Some have never heard of him at all, especially in the ages that preceded his incarnate ministry. Some who were born, and died in early infancy or childhood, have never been able to grasp the fullness of him and his salvation message. Many, even as adults, have not heard, to any significant level, the good news of salvation in Christ, or they were only poorly and partially taught, which robbed them of real salvation and spiritual opportunity in their day.

We are aware of the occasional exceptions to the rule when those such as Ruth, Rahab, Bathsheba and even Nebuchadnezzar exhibited faith in the

---

[3] *Sharon L. Baker, Razing Hell. (Louisville, Westminster John Knox Press, 2010), 12-13.*

true God. Though Nebuchadnezzar seemed to understand the greatness of Daniel's God it seems that he continued to honor and worship his traditional pagan deities as well. My point is that relatively few Gentiles came to have faith in the God of Israel in pre-Christian days.

It seems then, that there must be some adequate provision for those who had not heard the gospel, were not drawn to the worship of the true God and who were never taught the message and way of salvation. This book will seek to answer the question of how these souls, along with other unconverted people through the ages, who may have died in infancy and those who were poorly taught the gospel, may yet in spite of their ignorance, be granted the message of salvation and a moment of decision. If their salvific conversion does not occur in our age, then certainly it will be made available to them in the general resurrection during the eschaton.

In Scripture we see demonstration that God was not revealing himself to all the nations during the Old Testament era. He disclosed himself only to Israel. If they did not hear because of God's decided neglect of those peoples and generations, then how could he possibly, with any justice, condemn those whom he deliberately overlooked and kept in ignorance?

> Psalm 147:19 – 20 He declares His words to Jacob, His statutes and His ordinances to Israel. He has not dealt thus with any nation; and as for His ordinances, they have not known them. Praise the Lord! [4]

In near universally complete ignorance, the sons of men stand before the throne of God not knowing him, being unaware of his plan, his judgment, his mercy, his grace and His plan of salvation. The study of this state ought to lead to humility and gratitude in the minds of those of us who are willing to explore its ramifications. Do we simply and automatically accept Augustinian condemnation of these ignorant souls? Do we blindly and by rote fall down and worship at the traditional altar of doctrinal damnation of these wretched beings, who for no fault of their own stand doomed to an eternity of hellish and painful suffering for the high crime of not knowing or never having been properly taught the truth of salvation?

After this study it is no longer possible for me to accept the traditional Christian dogma of eternal suffering, by relatively innocent and ignorant souls, for all eternity. The very thought of it dismisses the kindness, mercy and grace of our beneficent God.

Jesus does not deny us access to understanding himself except for very good reason. He knows that, in our human state, our depth of

---

[4] *Lockman Foundation, Note-Takers Bible, New American Standard – Updated Edition. (Anaheim, Foundation Publications, Inc., 1999). (Quotations throughout unless otherwise noted.)*

understanding has severe limitation, by his own design as our Creator. He also understands that knowing too much too soon is detrimental to us. Consequently, we read his statement spoken to the disciples on the eve of his crucifixion whereby he conveyed this loving approach:

> John 16:12 I have many more things to say to you, but you cannot bear them now.

Solomon, the wisest man who ever lived, aside from our Lord, wrote about this matter. He conveys the idea, that in spite of our ability and desire to discover, we will never come to complete and total understanding of the mental capability of God.

> Ecclesiastes 3:11 He has made everything appropriate in its time. He also has set eternity in their heart, yet so that man will not find out the work which God has done from the beginning even to the end.

On the other hand, it is apparent that the saved will continue to learn of and from God for all eternity. Yet, we will never completely discover the entirety of the depths of knowledge that he has treasured up in his personal being. We see that concept expressed in Jesus who desires to teach us. His teaching through all eternity will be progressively offered that we may know God more fully. However, we will never achieve complete knowledge and the ability to bear it all. Only slowly, but surely, will God open his riches of understanding and intelligence to us over time.

PAUL'S STATEMENT AT MARS' HILL

Since we are largely ignorant of the true nature, plan, requirements, and wisdom of God, what hope do we have of standing accepted before Him? Paul gives us a strong hint of the state of mankind before God's throne of judgment in Acts 17:30 – 31. In speaking largely to Gentile Greeks at the Areopagus in Athens, in the midst of the emblems of their pagan religion, Paul declares the unknown God to them. It is interesting that they do acknowledge that they are indeed ignorant regarding this very God since they refer to him as the "unknown god." He also makes this statement in relation to the coming righteous judgment.

> Therefore having overlooked the times of ignorance, God is now declaring to men that all people everywhere should repent, because He has fixed a day in which He will judge the world in righteousness through a Man whom He has appointed, having furnished proof to all men by raising Him from the dead.

In this statement by Paul, the Holy Spirit reveals an important and vital divine principle regarding the judgment of mankind. That vital divine principle is that God overlooks our ignorance. Unlike the courts of our land, where ignorance of the law is no excuse, in the court of God, ignorance of Scriptural law is a valid excuse.

If this principle is true, then the entire scheme of traditional Christian teaching on the judgment is brought into question. If those who have never heard or been properly exposed to the saving word of God, are ignorant of the truth and their own culpability before God, how can they stand condemned before Him? How is it then that many believe that infants must be baptized lest they succumb to some agent of infant death and be forever lost and burning in excruciating everlasting hell fire? How can they be condemned if they have never heard and have not attained an age of understanding?

Bruce Reichenbach understands the principle that one cannot be held accountable for what never came into our possession. If one has not been granted knowledge of salvation and how it may be attained or received, then there is absolutely no legitimacy to accountability for what one does not understand.

> To hold persons accountable, it must be possible for them to avoid that for which they are being held accountable. They must have been able not to have done the deed. But if people cannot do unless God gives them the desire and power to do, they cannot do other than they have done. God can hold them accountable only with respect to what he has given them.[5]

The church's traditional view on salvation accountability has its roots in the beliefs and writings of Augustine.[6] Augustine's view of original sin found in Adam and Eve the source of the basic depravity of human kind. That depravity has been passed on hereditarily to all human beings. Simply then, all human beings are infected with the sin of our original parents and upon birth we are all accounted as worthy of the death penalty for sin and rebellion against God. This concept of original sin, in the view of Augustine and his supporters, applies to any newborn whether the child has actually committed sin or not. In original sin we inherit a sinful nature and its associated guilt from our forbearers.[7]

This view of the sinful human condition was furthered in the teachings

---

[5] Bruce R. Reichenbach, *The Grace of God and the Will of Man*. Chapter Fifteen, Freedom, Justice, and Moral Responsibility. General Editor Clark H. Pinnock. (Minneapolis, Bethany House Publishers, 1989), 296 – 297.
[6] Saint Augustine, *City of God*. Translated by Henry Bettenson. (London, Penguin Books Group, 2003), 688 – 689.
[7] John S. Feinberg, *The Many Faces of Evil*. (Wheaton, Crossway Books, 2004), 68.

of Martin Luther and John Calvin. Since their day, both the Roman Catholic and principal Protestant denominations all have promoted the idea of original sin. This belief also affected their views on infant baptism. Since even innocent babies are sinners by nature because of their inheritance of original sin, then the church saw it to be vital to baptize infants before they would possibly succumb to an untimely death and be lost in the fires of hell for eternity having never received the sacrament of holy baptism for salvation. [8]

Ormerod concludes his discussion on the matter with the following statement:
> Perhaps the main element that remains from Augustine's case is the church's practice of baptizing infants. [9]

Though Arminianism has theological perspectives different from those of John Calvin, on the issues of infant baptism and original sin they both hold general agreement with Protestant orthodoxy on the matter of inherited sin. Roger E. Olson states this agreement in the following manner:
> Classical Arminianism agrees with Protestant orthodoxy in general that the unity of the human race in sin results in all being born "children of wrath." However, Arminians believe that Christ's death on the cross provides a universal remedy for the guilt of inherited sin so that it is not imputed to infants for Christ's sake. This is how Arminians, in agreement with Anabaptists, such as Mennonites, interpret the universalistic passages of the New Testament such as Romans 5, where all are said to be included under sin just as all are included in redemption through Christ. ......Arminian belief in general redemption is not universal salvation; it is universal redemption from Adam's sin. Thus, in Arminian theology all children who die before reaching the age of awakening of conscience and falling into actual sin (as opposed to inbred sin) are considered innocent by God and are taken to paradise. Among those who commit actual sins only those who repent and believe have Christ as Savior.[10]

To hold to a doctrine of eternal suffering for those who never really had opportunity to respond to the gospel, seems to be an absolutely heartless and graceless position, especially when it is confronted with a far more lenient and merciful nature on the part of the revealed God of the gospel. He does not hold us accountable for what we do not know.
> Romans 5:13 for until the Law sin was in the world, but sin is not imputed when there is no law.

---

[8] *John S. Feinberg, The Many Faces of Evil. (Wheaton, Crossway Books, 2004), 68.*
[9]*Neil Ormerod, Creation, Grace, and Redemption. (Maryknoll, NY., Orbis Books, 2007), 71.*
[10] *Roger E. Olson, Arminian Theology. (Downer's Grove, IVP Academic, 2006), 33.*

God overlooks our ignorance. John Feinberg states the case well.

> Any theistic position committed to the existence of hell seems out of touch with the times and seems bankrupt religiously, morally, and theologically. In the judgment of many, the traditional doctrine of hell is an embarrassment to those who hold it.[11]

Biblical truth regarding the judgment of God should not be and is in fact not an embarrassment for Christians. The judgment upon the pre-flood world is not an embarrassment. I will demonstrate in this work that those who were opposed to righteousness had their lives snuffed out but they are not continuing in eternal suffering today because in Scripture we see that they too were ignorant of the true word and purpose of God.

NOAH PREACHED RIGHTEOUSNESS

It is interesting to note that Noah is called "a preacher of righteousness" (2 Peter 2:5). During his day, while the ark was being prepared, it is apparent that Noah preached a message of salvation to the world in which he warned them to repent of their sins. Let it be of some comfort to those of us who are also preachers of righteousness that Noah did not make one single convert during all those years of preaching. In fact Scripture tells us that none of those who heard Noah preach really understood until the flood actually appeared, when it was obviously too late for them to be saved from that world-encompassing catastrophe.

> Matthew 24:39 and they did not understand until the flood came and took them all away; so will the coming of the Son of Man be.

The evil and wicked generation of Noah's day did not comprehend the true import of Noah's preaching until it was too late. As a consequence they lost their lives in that day. The real question is, are they lost for all eternity? That question is not answered in Matthew's gospel. In context, Jesus is speaking of the conditions that will be in existence at the time of his glorious return. That generation too, like Noah's contemporaries, will be unaware and ignorant.

Peter gives us a hint regarding their future spiritual salvation when he speaks regarding those who are currently dead, who had been taught of the gospel in the past. He notes that they are currently held in a state as "judged in the flesh as men," that is as sinners, "that they may"(future tense) yet "live in the spirit according to the will of God."

---

[11] *John S. Feinberg, The Many Faces of Evil. (Wheaton, Crossway Books, 2004), 396.*

> I Peter 4:6 for the gospel has for this purpose been preached even to those who are dead, that though they are judged in the flesh as men, they may live in the spirit according to the will of God.

It is God's will that they live. He wills that all men may be saved (I Timothy 2:4), even those of Noah's day and those of Sodom and Gomorrah. In this verse from Peter he seems to leave the door open to yet future salvation for those who are dead, who are currently judged as sinful men but who "may live in the spirit according to the will of God." In fact, the chief Apostle also explained that those who turn away from salvation in Christ after having known the truth will be worse off than those who never knew it. Certainly he understood that ignorance of the way of salvation does not lead to condemnation since it would be better for those who had not understood than for those who knew, accepted Christ and then later rejected him.

> 2 Peter 2:20 – 21 For if, after they have escaped the defilements of the world by the knowledge of the Lord and Savior Jesus Christ, they are again entangled in them and are overcome, the last state has become worse for them than the first. For it would be better for them not to have known the way of righteousness, than having known it, to turn away from the holy commandment handed on to them.

Jesus instructed His disciples as to how to go out and preach the gospel. Of those cities, which would not receive them or their message, they were to "shake the dust off your feet" (Matthew 10:14). Those cities then would face the coming judgment day being worse off than Sodom and Gomorrah.

> Matthew 10:15 Truly I say to you, it will be more tolerable for the land of Sodom and Gomorrah in the day of judgment than for that city.

Jesus seems to imply that Sodom and Gomorrah did not receive the powerful witness that the cities, which the disciples would cover, would receive. In other words, Sodom and Gomorrah were more ignorant than these cities would be. As a consequence it would be "more tolerable" for those ancient cities of the Patriarchal age in the judgment than it would be for those of Jesus' day.

This can become a confusing issue. If, according to mainstream theology, the residents of Sodom and Gomorrah are currently continuing to suffer in eternal hell fire, how then will it be more tolerable for them on the day of judgment than for the cities of Judea during Jesus' day? Will God turn down the thermostat in Sodom and Gomorrah's corner of hell so it will not be as hot? Is that how it will be "more tolerable?" Or did Jesus mean something totally different?

It is apparent that Jesus meant exactly what He said. When all of these people rise in the second resurrection to judgment they will be granted full opportunity to know the gospel, salvation in Christ, and everlasting life, if only they choose to accept it. If the Lord judges us according to our understanding, then these cities that were to be witnessed to by the disciples would know much more about salvation than Sodom and Gomorrah ever did. Consequently, judgment against relatively spiritually ignorant Sodom and Gomorrah would not be as demanding and seemingly harsh as it will be for those who would be better informed. In that way the judgment will "be more tolerable for the land of Sodom and Gomorrah."

Genesis 19 describes the horrible destruction of the cities of Sodom and Gomorrah. The Lord had sent fire and brimstone to consume those two exceedingly sinful cities and they have served as an example of the fiery wrath of God ever since.

> Genesis 19:27 – 28 Now Abraham arose early in the morning and went to the place where he had stood before the Lord; and he looked down toward Sodom and Gomorrah, and toward all the land of the valley, and he saw, and behold, the smoke of the land ascended like the smoke of a furnace.

And so for thousands of years the words "Sodom and Gomorrah" have served as a warning, an ominous sign of just what happens when God decides to judge swiftly and decisively.

But this isn't the last we read of Sodom and Gomorrah.

The prophet Ezekiel had a series of visions in which God shows him what's coming, including the promise that God will "restore the fortunes of Sodom and her daughters" and they will "return to what they were before" (chap. 16).

Restore the fortunes of Sodom? The story isn't over for Sodom and Gomorrah?

What appeared to be a final, forever, smoldering, smoking verdict regarding their destiny…wasn't? What appeared to be over, isn't. Ezekiel says that where there was destruction there will be restoration.

But that still isn't the last we hear of these two cities. As Jesus travels from village to village in Galilee, calling people to see things in a whole new way, he encounters great resistance in some areas, especially among the more religious and devout. In Matthew 10, he warns the people living in the village of Capernaum, "It will be more bearable for Sodom and Gomorrah on the day of judgment than for you."

> More bearable for Sodom and Gomorrah? He tells highly committed, pious, religious people that it will be better for Sodom and Gomorrah than them on judgment day?
>
> There's still hope? And if there's still hope for Sodom and Gomorrah, what does that say about all of the other Sodoms and Gomorrahs?[12]

In Ezekiel 16 the Lord speaks of the terrible sinfulness of his people and of the day in which Jerusalem, Sodom and Samaria will be restored from their captivity, presumably their captivity to sin and its deadly consequences, and that they will be restored to "their former state" (vs. 55). Not only will they be restored to life at the time of their resurrection, but Israel will also be restored to its former covenantal relationship with God (vs. 60) and in that restoration they will be brought to the understanding of their shameful sinful state, which is no better, in fact is worse than their sister Sodom. Not until then, when they finally come face to face their own shame, will they receive the accompanying judicial forgiveness from their gracious God. Only then will Israel be brought to the depth of humility that will cause them to never again speak against or to forsake their Lord because of their full recognition of their own personal and national sinfulness.

> Ezekiel 16:62 – 63 Thus I will establish My covenant with you, and you shall know that I am the Lord, so that you may remember and be ashamed and never open your mouth anymore because of your humiliation, when I have forgiven you for all that you have done, the Lord God declares.

Scripture continually focuses on the necessity of sinners recognizing their own sinfulness in a state of humility before they can receive the judicial application of the forgiveness and grace of God. This is but one more in a long string of such examples which include the call to repentance and confession of sin by John the Baptist in Matthew 3:2 & 6.

Paul's Ignorance

The apostle Paul had been one of the most highly educated and strongly religious men of first century Judaism. He had studied under the renowned doctor of the law, Gamaliel (Acts 5:34). Paul was zealous for God and for all the traditions of the elders. He was thoroughly schooled in the Scriptures but his education had not taught him to understand that salvation is available only through Jesus Christ. It was not until the Lord, Jesus the Nazarene,

---

[12] *Rob Bell, Love Wins. A Book About Heaven, Hell, And The Fate Of Every Person Who Ever Lived. (New York, Harper One, 2011) 83 – 85.*

struck him blind while he made his way on the road to Damascus to persecute the Christians, that Paul began to learn the full truth of salvation (Acts 22:6 – 8).

With all of Paul's education and his Hebrew Benjamite pedigree, Paul still did not know enough for salvation. Not until he came to humility, under the direction of the Lord Jesus, did Paul come to know salvation by faith through the grace of Jesus the Christ. In spite of his background, he understood in the end that he needed more.

> I Timothy 1:13 – 15 even though I was formerly a blasphemer and persecutor and a violent aggressor. Yet I was shown mercy because I acted ignorantly in unbelief. And the grace of our Lord was more than abundant, with the faith and love which are found in Christ Jesus. It is a trustworthy statement, deserving full acceptance, that Christ Jesus came into the world to save sinners, among whom I am foremost of all.

Paul clearly states that salvation for him came about by the mercy of God because of his ignorance. Could the divine nature respond only to Paul this way or could it be that all humanity is and will be dealt with in the same manner? Will God overlook our ignorance? Even in the Great White Throne Judgment, will there be allowance for lack of understanding?

Peter, the chief apostle, clarifies the matter by teaching that God showed him that salvation is available to people of all nations. Our pedigree and ancestry count for nothing in matters of salvation since God is not "a respecter of persons" (Acts 10:34 KJV).

In Peter's second sermon to the worshippers in Jerusalem, just following the festival of Pentecost, he utters the same principle we previously read which Paul would later expound. He points out to his hearers that they were responsible for the crucifixion and death of "the Prince of life" (Acts 3:15).

> Acts 3:12 – 16 But when Peter saw this, he replied to the people, 'Men of Israel, why are you amazed at this, or why do you gaze at us, as if by our own power or piety we had made him walk? The God of Abraham, Isaac and Jacob, the God of our fathers, has glorified His servant Jesus, the one whom you delivered and disowned in the presence of Pilate, when he had decided to release Him. But you disowned the Holy and Righteous One and asked for a murderer to be granted to you, but put to death the Prince of life, the one whom God raised from the dead, a fact to which we are witnesses. And on the basis of faith in His name, it is the name of Jesus which has strengthened this man whom you see and know; and the faith which comes through Him has given him this perfect health in the presence of you all.

Peter nevertheless, under inspiration of the Holy Spirit, overlooks the actions of the people on the basis of their ignorance. Not only does Peter excuse the crowd but he also acquits their rulers and calls upon them to repent (vs. 17-19).

> And now, brethren, I know that you acted in ignorance, just as your rulers did also. But the things which God announced beforehand by the mouth of all the prophets, that His Christ would suffer, he has thus fulfilled. Therefore repent and return, so that your sins may be wiped away, in order that times of refreshing may come from the presence of the Lord.

ONLY A SELECT FEW CAN UNDERSTAND

In Romans 11 Paul is speaking to Gentile converts to Christianity. He explains to these Gentiles that their salvation has been made possible at that time because of the temporary condition of the hardening of the hearts of most of the people of Israel. According to his words, when the Gentiles fully come to salvation, then and only then will the doors reopen so that the near universal salvation of Israel can take place. They will finally be aroused out of their spiritual stupor and will be driven to jealousy (vs. 11) in finally accepting the Lord Jesus as their Savior and God. Paul's desire and inspired statement regarding his own people is: "and so all Israel will be saved (vs. 26)."

It is notable that Jesus did not want all people to come to salvation in his day. When the disciples questioned why he only spoke to the crowds in parables and not in plain statements regarding the kingdom of God, he answered in a manner that seems to be an enigma to many.

> Matthew 13:11 Jesus answered them, 'To you it has been granted to know the mysteries of the kingdom of heaven, but to them it has not been granted.'

By God's sovereign decision, these crowds were not being allowed to have their minds illuminated to the spiritual intent of Jesus' teaching. By God's choice they were being kept ignorant of the way of salvation. He could speak to them but they would not understand. This concept was affirmed by both Jesus and by the prophet Isaiah.

> Matthew 13:13 – 15 Therefore I speak to them in parables; because while seeing they do not see, and while hearing they do not hear, nor do they understand. In their case the prophecy of Isaiah is being fulfilled, which says, 'You will keep on hearing, but will not understand; you will keep on seeing, but will not perceive; for the heart of this people has become dull, with their ears they scarcely

> hear, and they have closed their eyes, otherwise they would see with their eyes, hear with their ears, and understand with their heart and return, and I would heal them.'

But there were a select few who did understand and they included the disciples. Jesus' disciples were allowed to see, hear and understand.

> (vs. 16 – 17) But blessed are your eyes, because they see; and your ears, because they hear. For truly I say to you that many prophets and righteous men desired to see what you see, and did not see it, and to hear what you hear, and did not hear it.

Mark further elaborates on this same question in chapter four, verses ten to twelve. He makes the bold statement that the people do not perceive or understand, "otherwise they might repent and be forgiven."

> As soon as He was alone, His followers, along with the twelve, began asking Him about the parables. And He was saying to them, 'To you has been given the mystery of the kingdom of God, but those who are outside get everything in parables, so that while seeing, they may see, and not perceive, and while hearing, they may hear and not understand, otherwise they might return and be forgiven.'

If Jesus is in the business of saving souls from hell, why does he not want all people to understand and to "repent and be forgiven?" Could it possibly be that this age is not the only God-ordained time for all mankind to come to salvation? In that case, and since he desires that all men be saved, why does he not automatically make salvation available to everyone now and grant them the open-mindedness to be able to accept it? After all, Paul assures us that God "desires all men to be saved and to come to the knowledge of the truth (I Timothy 2:4)."

If all these Scriptures are true and inspired by the Holy Spirit, can all these statements be true, or perhaps only some of them? Or perhaps we do not understand the design and salvation plan of God very well. It is the purpose of this volume to reexamine our traditional theology on this important issue of salvation.

Peter acknowledged an excuse for the Judean persecutors who executed Jesus. They were ignorant of what they were doing. In Acts 3:17 he makes that allowance abundantly plain. "And now brethren, I know that you acted in ignorance, just as your rulers did also."

In this statement he excuses, at least to some degree, their culpability regarding Jesus' crucifixion. The responsibility of their rulers is also overlooked. Nevertheless, once they have come to the knowledge of the truth, then and only then does God expect that they "repent and return, so that your sins may be wiped away (vs. 19)." We are not held responsible for sin until we have come to the knowledge of the requirements of God.

> Hebrews 6:4 – 6 For in the case of those who have once been enlightened and have tasted of the heavenly gift and have been made partakers of the Holy Spirit, and have tasted the good word of God and the powers of the age to come, and then have fallen away, it is impossible to renew them again to repentance, since they again crucify to themselves the Son of God and put Him to open shame..... (10:26) For if we go on sinning willfully after receiving the knowledge of the truth, there no longer remains a sacrifice for sins, but a terrifying expectation of judgment and the fury of a fire which will consume the adversaries.

SINS COMMITTED IN IGNORANCE

It is also interesting to note in the book of Hebrews that God made allowance, even in the Old Testament sacrificial system, for sins committed in ignorance. On the day of Atonement, the only day of the year that any human being could enter into the Holy of Holies in the temple, and only the High Priest at that, the High Priest was to make an offering to the Lord on behalf of himself and the people for their sins committed in ignorance.

> Hebrews 9:7 but into the second, only the high priest enters once a year, not without taking blood, which he offers for himself and for the sins of the people committed in ignorance.

Without a doubt, the Lord is interested in forgiving us for committing sins and even our neglect of him out of ignorance. He made a sacrificial allowance for it in the Old Testament, and certainly he made a sacrificial allowance on Calvary for us in the New Testament context as well. That allowance for our ignorance was made in one of the last seven pronouncements of our Lord while on the cross.

FATHER FORGIVE THEM FOR THEY KNOW NOT WHAT THEY DO

Jesus himself illustrated the principle of overlooking ignorance while he was in the process of suffering the excruciating pain of the crucifixion. When the Roman soldiers stripped him bare, nailed his wrists to the crossbeam, his feet to the stake and as they began to gamble for his only remaining personal possession, his seamless and expensive festival clothing. Jesus then cried out with his first prayer from atop Golgotha, "Father, forgive them; for they do not know what they are doing. (Luke 23:34)" In making that statement Jesus is himself pardoning and excusing their murderous behavior. They were ignorant of who he was. They were ignorant of the salvation that was offered through his patient kindness and his expression of abundant grace even to them.

According to the prophet Zechariah, Jesus is predicted to come again to meet face to face with his executioners. After his return at the second coming, even those who executed him will come to see him directly as he will appear in his glory. Revelation 1:7 is a quotation from the fuller treatment given the subject in Zechariah 12:10 – 13:9.

> Behold He is coming with the clouds, and every eye will see Him, even those who pierced Him; and all the tribes of the earth will mourn over Him. So it is to be. Amen.

According to Jesus' statement on the cross, those who pierced him are granted forgiveness. Their sin of murder is overlooked because of their ignorance. They will not be judged for it nor for their actions. But it is easy to discern that even though they are forgiven, nevertheless they are to be filled with remorse and will be given a heart of "grace and supplication" in repentance before God.

> Zechariah 12:10 I will pour out on the house of David and on the inhabitants of Jerusalem, the spirit of grace and of supplication, so that they will look on Me whom they have pierced; and they will mourn for Him, as one mourns for an only son, and they will weep bitterly over Him like the bitter weeping over a firstborn.

We see in this case that the Lord's preemptive forgiveness in advance of judgment still produces the desired result of repentance, which leads to salvation. This principle is at work regarding Paul's correspondence with the church at Corinth. His first letter was rather corrective on a number of issues, and in the second letter he notes with joy how they were moved by that epistle to a state of repentance. Not only were they moved to repentance, but that repentance also led to their salvation.

> 2 Corinthians 7:9–10 I now rejoice, not that you were made sorrowful, but that you were made sorrowful to the point of repentance; for you were made sorrowful according to the will of God, so that you might not suffer loss in anything through us. For the sorrow that is according to the will of God produces a repentance without regret, leading to salvation, but the sorrow of the world produces death.

If the repentance of the Corinthian Church in Paul's day led to the salvation of the congregation, can we expect anything less for those who pierced Jesus to be granted salvation as a result of their repentance in the judgment yet to come? If the time of repentance is limited to this current age and life, then those who never heard or were ignorant of the way of salvation in this life would have nothing but a frustrating redundant statement of condemnation to look forward to hearing at the post-millennial judgment. If the unrighteous dead are at this very moment suffering the pain of eternal torment, then just what divine purpose would be accomplished if they were resurrected simply to have their sins recounted and judgment and sentence restated, if they have no opportunity to repent with the end result of salvation? There is evidence in Scripture, to which this treatise is dedicated, for an entirely different and clearly more merciful end than what is offered to us in the doctrines of traditional Christian Theology.

QUALIFICATIONS OF A PASTOR

One of the most important qualifications for any pastor or priest in the human realm is the same major qualification that Jesus has as our divine High Priest. That major qualification centers on the concepts of mercy and grace in consideration of the frailties of the human condition of those he is to serve.

> Hebrews 5:1 – 3 For every high priest taken from among men is appointed on behalf of men in things pertaining to God, in order to offer both gifts and sacrifices for sins; he can deal gently with the ignorant and misguided, since he himself also is beset with weakness; and because of it he is obligated to offer sacrifices for sins, as for the people, so also for himself.

Jesus exemplifies this approach to us. He is our High Priest. He is qualified to be our High Priest, in part because he humbled himself, became one of us, lived as one of us, suffered as we do and learned from his own human fleshly limitations. Consequently he is able to deal with us and our frailties out of his own personal knowledge, experience, and his own difficult trials associated with human existence. The writer of Hebrews expresses the compassion of Jesus elegantly and beautifully in chapter four, verses 15 – 16:

> For we do not have a high priest who cannot sympathize with our weaknesses, but One who has been tempted in all things as we are, yet without sin. Therefore let us draw near with confidence to the throne of grace, so that we may receive mercy and find grace to help in time of need.

Can there be any doubt that Jesus is going to be a compassionate and considerate adjudicator at the final judgment? If he is compassionate, then will he not offer salvation to the repentant in that day?

Is This The Only Day Of Salvation?

The argument can be made that this is the one and only day of salvation. But is that reasoning actually biblical? Is this truly the only day of salvation?

2 Corinthians 6:2 is often cited as evidence and a proof-text for the concept that this is the only day of salvation. On the other hand, Peter points out that this current day is the day of judgment for those of us who are of the household of God. In fact, the day of judgment begins first with us, not with the whole world.

> I Peter 4:17 For it is time for judgment to begin with the household of God; and if it begins with us first, what will be the outcome for those who do not obey the gospel of God?

Paul's quotation of Isaiah 49 is incomplete. His parenthetical quotation is meant to stress the urgency of the moment.[13] The passage comes from the Septuagint, which slightly and yet significantly alters the source meaning of the concept. Isaiah 49 speaks of multiple days of salvation. The focus there is not on one singular day but of "*a day* of salvation" rather than "*the day* of salvation" as it is to Paul. Isaiah clearly indicates more than one singular day of salvation opportunity.

> Isaiah 49:8a Thus says the Lord, 'In a favorable time I have answered You, and in a day of salvation I have helped You; and I will keep You and give You for a covenant of the people,'

John's gospel sheds further light on the subject of the day of salvation in 12:47 – 48. In this passage he states that the day of judgment for the wicked will be on the last day, not "today."

> If anyone hears My sayings and does not keep them, I do not judge him: for I did not come to judge the world, but to save the world. He who rejects Me and does not receive My sayings, has one who judges him; the word I spoke is what will judge him at the last day. For I did not speak on My own initiative, but the Father Himself who sent Me has given Me a commandment as to what to say and what to speak.

The writer of Hebrews testifies that the final judgment will not come to completion until all people have been given full "knowledge of the truth." In his grace and mercy, God will not pronounce his sentence on the ungodly until they have made the deliberate and conscious decision to reject both him and his offer of salvation.

---

[13] *Ralph P. Martin, 2 Corinthians. (Nashville, Thomas Nelson Publishers, 1986), 167.*

> Hebrews 10:26 – 29 For if we go on sinning willfully after receiving the knowledge of the truth, there no longer remains a sacrifice for sins, but a terrifying expectation of judgment and the fury of a fire which will consume the adversaries. Anyone who has set aside the Law of Moses dies without mercy on the testimony of two or three witnesses. How much severer punishment do you think he will deserve who has trampled under foot the Son of God, and has regarded as unclean the blood of the covenant by which he was sanctified, and has insulted the Spirit of grace?

Notice that the freely offered sacrifice of Jesus Christ, to pay the penalty of our sins, will be fully withdrawn from those who consciously, with full knowledge, continue willfully in their sin and rebellion against the sovereign God. Such willful rejection can only be accomplished after having received full instruction and knowledge of the gospel. Such rejection indeed merits death, annihilation, and eternal separation from the Savior.

In rebellion, that irreconcilable sinner has rejected the authority of the Father and the saving sacrifice of the Son as well as insulting the Holy Spirit's grace. Such a one, by his own choice, would be a candidate for annihilation in the Lake of Fire, according to Revelation 20:15.

> And if anyone's name was not found written in the book of life, he was thrown into the lake of fire.

On the other hand, undoubtedly this group of incorrigibles will be very small. As a whole, it is difficult to conceive that most people, or even a large minority, would not choose salvation in Christ. Once enlightened after the general second resurrection, it is entirely conceivable that the vast majority of mankind will come to salvation. They will readily respond when finally they receive complete education pertaining to salvation.

Those who in this life never heard the gospel, died as infants or in childhood not having attained an age of accountability, and those who were simply inadequately taught, or who were never taught at all, are not going to be abandoned to eternal suffering or annihilation in a poorly conceived doctrine of hell. God is entirely too fair and merciful to ever allow that condition to be enforced upon such unfortunate souls, who are after all, his own children.

David Powys speaks of the position of Western Christendom at the time of the Reformation regarding the fate of believers and unbelievers. Orthodoxy at that time essentially espoused Augustine's position, which had been sanctioned by the Fourth Lateran Council, regarding everlasting torment that awaited the reprobate. The council, speaking of the coming judgment, determined this:

> He shall come at the end of time to judge the living and the dead and to render to each according to his works, to the reprobate as well as to the elect. All of them will rise again with their own bodies which they now bear, to receive according to their works, whether these have been good or evil, the ones perpetual punishment with the devil, and the others everlasting glory with Christ.[14]

It is apparent that Protestant Christianity derives much of its view regarding salvation, or the lack thereof for mankind, from ancient traditional teachings that were heavily influenced by Greek philosophy rather than from Scripture itself. That is amazing because the battle cry of the reformers was *sola scriptura*, and yet Protestant churches today seem to have bowed at the altar of traditional Roman Catholic teachings on this vitally important subject. Do we have such a poor case for Christianity that we must resort almost exclusively to scaring people to death with the possibility of eternal hell fire to get them to come to church and to establish a relationship with God? Are we only selling fire insurance, or is the genuine gospel in its positive and wonderful ramifications in need of far greater presentation than we have given it?

The message of the gospel is far more encouraging than we seem able to convey. The first-century apostles of Christ preached about the ministry, the death and resurrection and the coming return of Christ, which make possible the resurrection, the regeneration to eternal life of all believers. Positive news as opposed to "scaring the hell out of people." It is true that far too much of what passes for the gospel today focuses on avoiding the eternal suffering of hell. Shouldn't we rather be teaching the Scriptural truth that believers will be the "bride of Christ" and that they will be granted rulership as "kings and priests" forever with Jesus? Could our teaching perhaps better focus on the idea that in Christ one can have his tranquility and peace in this insane world that offers only confusion, stress and painful difficulty? These are far more positive focal points that we ought to be teaching.

Edward Fudge describes how the traditional view ignores much of Scripture on the subject of salvation. He identifies one of the major problems in Christian teaching as involving the matter of the immortality of the soul and how it forces doctrine to do something with the immortal souls of the wicked. Consequently in ecclesiastical tradition, the only place the theologians have to locate the incorrigibly wicked, who inconveniently have immortal souls, is in an ever-burning and ever-torturous eternal hell.[15]

---

[14] *David Powys, 'Hell': A Hard Look at a Hard Question. (Milton Keynes, UK, 1997), 17*
[15] *Edward William Fudge, The Fire That Consumes. (Milton Keynes, UK., Paternoster Press, 2005), Introduction, xii.*

Scripture does not describe or promote such an existence. In fact the word of God presents a far more kind and merciful God than the traditionalists do. Jesus, in his ministry, described much better treatment for those who do not understand or never received the gospel in a manner that makes sense to them than what many of our preachers do today.

IF YOU WERE BLIND YOU WOULD HAVE NO SIN

After Jesus healed the man who had been born blind, he spoke to him and to the Pharisees regarding the matter of blindness. This healing episode had opened the door to such discussion and the Lord told them plainly one of the major reasons why he had come into the world.

> John 9:39 And Jesus said, 'For judgment I came into this world, so that those who do not see may see, and that those who see may become blind.'

In this case it is easy to see Jesus' reference to the physical blindness of the man being healed but it is also quite apparent that he was speaking not only of physical blindness but also, and most importantly, of spiritual blindness. There was no judgment to be applied to this healed man since his condition of blindness had been imposed upon him from birth. In fact, when asked about that by his disciples, Jesus made a plain statement that indicated that it was by God's sovereign will that this man was born blind in order that God may be glorified.

> John 9:1 – 3 As he passed by, He saw a man blind from birth. And His disciples asked Him, 'Rabbi, who sinned, this man or his parents, that he would be born blind?' Jesus answered, 'It was neither that this man sinned, nor his parents; but it was so that the works of God might be displayed in him.'

Is it possible that we also have specially designed flaws of body and soul that were created by God for his omniscient purpose? Of course it is possible. Pharaoh had no choice in the matter of his hardness of heart since it was divinely imposed upon him in order that God, through the whole experience, would be honored and glorified.

> Exodus 14:4 Thus I will harden Pharaoh's heart, and he will chase after them; and I will be honored through Pharaoh and all his army, and the Egyptians will know that I am the Lord.

In essence, Pharaoh had no choice in this matter of his heart's hardening. This was a condition imposed on him by God. In the judgment yet to come, how can God justifiably condemn Pharaoh for that change of heart when God himself forced it upon him? In the final judgment the Lord will have mercy on Pharaoh and will not judge him for either his ignorance nor for his hardness of heart since God's sovereign will inflicted the implacable heart upon Pharaoh for his own divine purpose. Not only Pharaoh, but consider all of his soldiers, relatively innocent in the matter, but still under his authority, who all died as a result of obedience to his orders. In a direct manner all of those soldiers died according to the will of God in order for the Lord to bring glory to himself. If God is not a malicious sadist, then all of those who died in that episode must be granted, in the future, a real opportunity for salvation. I believe that in the second resurrection judgment period this very opportunity will be offered to them and also to all mankind who never really had an informed choice to make regarding salvation through faith in Jesus Christ.

The book of Revelation speaks, in chapter twenty and verse six, of the first resurrection, which automatically implies a second resurrection. The first is for believers and the second resurrection and general judgment is spoken of in verses 11 – 15.

> (vs. 6) Blessed and holy is the one who has a part in the first resurrection; over these the second death has no power, but they will be priests of God and of Christ and will reign with Him for a thousand years

> (vss. 11 – 15) Then I saw a great white throne and Him who sat upon it, from whose presence earth and heaven fled away and no place was found for them. And I saw the dead, the great and the small, standing before the throne, and books were opened; and another book was opened, which is the book of life; and the dead were judged from the things which were written in the books, according to their deeds. And the sea gave up the dead which were in it, and death and Hades gave up the dead which were in them; and they were judged, every one of them according to their deeds. Then death and Hades were thrown into the lake of fire. This is the second death, the lake of fire. And if anyone's name was not found written in the book of life, he was thrown into the lake of fire.

God judges us out of our own mouths. If we claim understanding then God will judge us based on that understanding. The Pharisees were the principal religious leaders of the day. They claimed to know the Scriptures and had very strict rules as to how the law of Moses was to be applied. In Jesus' discussion with them, regarding the man born blind, we find an important principle, which governs our guilt or innocence before God.

> John 9:40 – 41 Those of the Pharisees who were with Him heard these things and said to him, 'We are not blind too, are we?' Jesus

> said to them, 'If you were blind you would have no sin; but since you say, 'We see,' your sin remains.

This is an astounding statement by Jesus. "If you were blind you would have no sin." Can we take any other interpretation from that sentence other than the fact that spiritual ignorance is overlooked in judgment? Spiritual blindness is a trump card in the consideration of our standing before the throne of God. He will not judge us based on what we do not know but rather on what we do understand or maintain that we understand.

Jesus again spoke of the matter of one's ignorance in John 15:20 – 24. In the upper room on his last night before the crucifixion he warned them that if his enemies had persecuted him they would persecute the disciples as well. He went on to explain why the religious leaders were without excuse for their persecutions of himself and ultimately of the disciples.

> Remember the word that I said to you,' A slave is not greater than his master. ' If they persecuted Me they will also persecute you; if they kept My word, they will keep yours also. But all these things they will do to you for My name's sake, because they do not know the One who sent Me. If I had not come and spoken to them, they would not have sin, but now they have no excuse for their sin. He who hates Me hates My Father also. If I had not done among them the works which no one else did, they would not have sin; but now they have both seen and hated Me and My Father as well.

Herein Jesus again gives great insight into the matter of accountability for sin. He expresses the truism that since he came and spoke to them, and likewise in his entire ministry of conducting healings and miracles and teaching the word of God in power and authority, he witnessed the works of God to them. Therefore the persecutors are without excuse. On the contrary, if he had not spoken the word to them or conducted the works of God in their presence then they would have had an excuse. In this example we can see how those who never really got the gospel preached to them or were improperly taught, shall have opportunity for salvation in the judgment because they did not know better. They had not been truly reached with a salvation opportunity in this life. The Pharisees and other religious leaders had been witnessed to by Christ. They were then truly without excuse for their sins.

In the case of the Pharisees, their claim of understanding removed excuse from them for their evil behavior and misguided teaching. Yet even in their claim to know, they did not really understand. So it seems they too, in their genuine spiritual blindness, were included in Jesus' prayer on Golgotha, "Father forgive them; for they do not know what they are doing."

In Romans 11 the Apostle Paul writes of Israel being partially hardened to the gospel and understanding of God's plan of salvation. We see that hardness came about as a result of their obstinate disobedience (10:21). But even in that hardened condition the plan of God is not thwarted. God's intent is to bring Israel back to relationship with himself by making them jealous that the Gentiles have come to salvation instead of Israel. When could Israel possibly come to such jealousy and salvation as a whole? Only in the context of the future general resurrection and the judgment period when they shall become painfully aware that God has brought the Gentiles to salvation and that salvation is available only through faith in Jesus the Lord, whom they had previously rejected.

> Romans 11:11 I say then, they did not stumble so as to fall, did they? May it never be! But by their transgression salvation has come to the Gentiles, to make them jealous.

In spite of Israel's temporary hardness of heart, Israel will finally come to salvation, and not just a few, not just one generation, but like Ezekiel 37 pictures, the whole house of Israel will be resurrected back to life and salvation (Ezekiel 37:11 – 14).

> Romans 11:25 – 27 For I do not want you, brethren, to be uninformed of this mystery – so that you will not be wise in your own estimation – that a partial hardening has happened to Israel until the fullness of the Gentiles has come in; and so all Israel will be saved; just as it is written, "The Deliverer will come from Zion, he will remove ungodliness from Jacob. This is My covenant with them, when I take away their sins."

Lloyd Gaston, in the book *The Romans Debate*, sees the hardening and blindness of Israel as being an act of God. He does so not to disinherit his people but rather as a temporary condition in order that they may finally come to salvation.

> The vast majority were blinded but blinded by God, to fulfill his purposes, both for Israel and for Gentiles. The rest are not repudiated, and their blinding is not a punishment but part of God's action for salvation. It has been a longstanding assumption that Paul uses the remnant concept in order to disinherit Israel. That is not the case.[16]

Clearly, God's intent regarding Israel is to restore them to covenantal relationship with himself and to "take away their sins." This individual and collective restoration of Israel will not and cannot take place until the general resurrection. This is a yet future event on a grand scale.

---

[16] *Lloyd Gaston, The Romans Debate. Karl P. Donfried, Editor.(Peabody, Hendrickson Publishers, LLC, 2005), 318.*

We cannot further the idea of Conditional Immortality without also considering the matter of the state of the soul. If, as mainstream Christian traditional theology maintains, the soul is immortal, then all souls will spend eternity either in heavenly bliss or in hellish suffering. Under the same theological perspective all souls are also consigned to either of those two options immediately upon death. In that case there is no room for further opportunity for repentance and acceptance of salvation in Christ beyond this life.

The Conditionalist view presents the biblical prospect of opportunity for salvation beyond this present mortal life. In that case, there is a need for further instruction during the eschatonal judgment, regarding the gospel and Christian education for those who did not have such an option in this present age to accept the salvation offered in the Lord. If the soul is mortal, and is non-existent in the intermediate state after physical death, then it is possible to develop a theology that allows for their further instruction after the general resurrection from the dead. This will be the focus in Chapter Three as we explore various perspectives regarding the state of the soul.

CHAPTER THREE
MAN'S MORTALITY

Chapter Three

Man's Mortality

*Much of the soul they talk,
but all awry.*[17]

We now consider whether man's soul is mortal or immortal. If the soul is immortal, then we must spend the intermediate state, after death and before the resurrection, alive somewhere because we are eternally existent in that case. On the other hand, if our souls are mortal, we are then simply metaphorically asleep in the grave awaiting our anticipated resurrection at the eschaton.

The Origin Of The Soul In Scripture

The first mention of "soul" in Scripture is found in Genesis 2:7 (KJV) regarding the creation of Adam. The book of Genesis by its very name is a book of beginnings. Consequently, the beginning of Scripture's discussion of matters of the soul originates in this foundational first book of the Pentateuch. In 2:7 we see a formula for the creation of the soul, which in its brevity and economy of words, is not equaled elsewhere in the Bible.

> And the Lord God formed man of the dust of the ground, and breathed into his nostrils the breath of life, and man became a living soul. (KJV)

In more modern translations the term "soul" is translated as "living being" such as in the NAS. This translation reduces some of the sense of the ethereal metaphysical spiritual nature that can seem to be implied in the term "soul."

> Then the Lord God formed man of dust of the ground, and breathed into his nostrils the breath of life; and man became a living being.

It is well worth dissecting this passage in order to have a greater depth of understanding as to what exactly occurred in this most important act of creation. First, we notice that the soul or living being is the product of the combination of two essential elements. Man, as a living being, is partially the product of the physical corpse, which consists of the material elements of the dust of the earth. In addition, the purely material corpse is then infused with the very breath of God. Only after these two basic elements

---

[17] *John Milton, Paradise Regained, (1671), IV, 313.*

are conjoined by the Creator does the corpse come to animate life and is then referred to as a "soul" or "living being."

In this abbreviated explanation of the creation of man one can see that the biblical soul is the combination of both physical material elements and the spiritual breath of God. George Eldon Ladd gives further insight into the matter of the soul:

> Soul (*nepes*) is not a higher part of humanity standing over against the body but designates the vitality or life principle in a person. God breathed into Adam's nostrils the breath of life, and he became a living *nepes* (Gen. 2:7). Body and the divine breath together make the vital, active *nepes*. The word is then extended from the life principle to include the feelings, passions, will, and even the mentality of the individual. It then comes to be used as a synonym for humanity itself. Families were numbered as so many souls (Gen. 12:5; 46:27). Incorporeal life for the *nepes* is never visualized. Death afflicted the *nepes* (Num. 23:10) as well as the body.[18]

Robert Leo Odom indicates that man's soul is his temporary physical life. In addition he also sees that Genesis 2:7 does not at all further the idea that man's soul or life is immortal.

> Note particularly that the Sacred Record does not say that God breathed into man's nostrils a soul. He breathed into the first man's nostrils "the breath of life" and then "man became a living soul." Note, too, that it does not say that man became an immortal soul.[19]

While pagan philosophy sees the soul as metaphysical and completely immaterial in nature, the biblical soul is both spirit and matter in perfect combination. This point is made by Oscar Cullman as he sees that both the body and soul are created by God and are both good. This goodness is opposed to Greek dualistic philosophy which sees the body as evil and only the soul as good, awaiting the time of its release from the evil bodily prison at death. [20]

Additionally, Thomas F. Torrance gives us understanding regarding the three major traditions which have had a powerful impact on our views regarding the soul. He emphasizes the dualism of the Greek and Roman

---

[18] George Eldon Ladd, *A Theology of the New Testament*. (Grand Rapids, William Eerdman's Publishing Company, 2002), 500.
[19] Robert Leo Odom, *Is Your Soul Immortal?* (Ukiah, CA., Orion Publishing, 2007), 10.
[20] Oscar Cullmann, *Immortality of the Soul or Resurrection of the Dead?* (London, The Epworth Press, 1958), 30.

views while citing the idea that the Hebrew Scriptures support the unity of the body and spirit in forming the soul.

> The three great traditions have contributed to the image of man prevailing in western thought: the Greek, the Roman, and the Hebrew. Greek and Roman views of humanity were both governed, although in somewhat different ways, by a radical dualism of body and soul (or mind), the soul being regarded as but loosely related to the body in which it is temporally imprisoned. The Hebrew view of humanity, on the other hand, was distinctly non-dualist, for man's body and soul were regarded as forming an integrated unity, with man's body as body of his soul and his soul as soul of his body.[21]

Josef Pieper speaks of how Socrates confirmed among his friends the philosophic idea that at death and dying that "nothing other than the separation of soul from body"[22] takes place. In biblical theology there is quite the contrary stated. The soul is the combination of the body and the spirit of God, *neshama*. It is that combination which constitutes the soul. The soul is not separate from the body but rather is partially consistent of it in combination with the breath of God. We are then living beings, or souls, when the breath of God and the lifeless body are brought into unity.

> Note the sequence of the steps in the process of the creation of man: *First*, man was made of the dust of the ground. *Second*, God breathed into his lifeless body the breath (*neshamah*) of life. The *result*: "Man became a living soul [*nephesh*]."[23]

The biblical teaching on the soul is quite different from that of the Greeks. The Bible advances the idea that the presence of both the body and spirit of God in union creates a living human being who is then only lacking the indwelling of the Holy Spirit to bring the living being into full communion with God and with eternal salvation.

> Body and soul are both originally good in so far as they are created by God; they are both bad in so far as the deadly power of the flesh has hold of them. Both can and must be set free by the quickening power of the Holy Spirit.[24]

The early church was beset with philosophical teaching of Greek and Eastern Mystical origin. The Apostle Paul spends a good deal of time in

---

[21] Thomas F. Torrance, *The Christian Frame Of Mind*. (Colorado Springs, Helmers & Howard, 1989), 35.
[22] Josef Pieper, *Death And Immortality*. (South Bend, Augustine Press, 2000), 23.
[23] Robert Leo Odom, *Is Your Soul Immortal?* (Ukiah, CA., Orion Publishing, 2007), 36.
[24] Josef Pieper, *Death And Immortality*. (South Bend, Augustine Press, 2000), 23.

his epistles combating such heretical influence that was creeping into the church even in his time in the developmental first century.

> Colossians 2:18, and 20 – 23 Let no one keep defrauding you of your prize by delighting in self-abasement and the worship of the angels, taking his stand on visions he has seen, inflated without cause by his fleshly mind…If you have died with Christ to the elementary principles of the world, why, as if you were living in the world, do you submit yourself to decrees, such as, "Do not handle, do not taste, do not touch!" (which all refer to things destined to perish with use) – in accordance with the commandments and teachings of men? These are matters which have, to be sure, the appearance of wisdom in self-made religion and self-abasement and severe treatment of the body, but are of no value against fleshly indulgence.

Clearly, Greek philosophy and Eastern Mysticism were strong influences, not only in the Jewish Church, but especially in the growing Gentile branch of Christianity, in the first century. Stewart Dingwall Fordyce Salmond helps us to understand the effect of philosophy and mysticism in his comments on the Hindu doctrine of the transmigration of the soul and its effect on the traditions of Christian teaching.

> When once it was accepted, it seems never to have been questioned. The various systems of philosophy occupied themselves with it. They taught that men's deeds lived after them and bore fruit, and therefore, that a succession of births must be. But they claimed at the same time to open up ways of deliverance. The Vedantist sages professed that, by the wisdom which they had to impart, a man's "works" could be neutralized or destroyed, so that nothing should remain to make a rebirth necessary, or to preclude the final happiness which had to wait for the exhaustion of these "works." And the masses of the people were under the spell of the same doctrine, finding in it, perhaps, some explanation of the inequalities of life, perhaps at times even a measure of solace in the miseries of life, but for the most part oppressed by its terror.

> In a way, therefore, which we can at the best but dimly surmise, the Hindu came to think of his soul as in a sense eternal as well as immortal. Its existence in any particular man in any particular generation of earth, was but an incident in its history. It had existed previously, and it would exist afterwards in some other man, some god, some animal, or some inanimate thing. It was so associated with the ideas of form and occupancy, that the thought of a disembodied existence for it was scarcely entertained. In the

> multitude of bodies through which it was to pass, each successive form of existence, whether it was to be high or low, of greater or less degree of trial and misery, was determined by its deeds in the preceding; and nay unworthy thing to which the soul might commit itself in any one of those interminable passing modes of existence, brought it down from any height of attainment to which it might have painfully struggled.[25]

In this passage Salmond gives us good understanding of the origin of the immortality of the soul as it came into Christianity from Hindu theology permeating and filtered through the philosophy of the Greeks. The soul was seen to be immortal and transmigrational as it passed from one being to another, generation after generation.

M. E. Osterhaven admits to this phenomenon of the power of foreign philosophy regarding the early church. Particularly noted is the influence of the teachings of Plato.

> Speculation about the soul in the subapostolic church was heavily influenced by Greek philosophy. This is seen in Origen's acceptance of Plato's doctrine of the preexistence of the soul as pure mind (nous) originally, which, by reason of its fall from God, cooled down to soul (psyche) when it lost its participation in the divine fire by looking earthward. It is also seen in Tertullian's repudiation of Greek ideas and his insistence on the biblical teaching of the union of the soul, an immaterial creation of God, with the material body which has been made for it.[26]

Donald Guthrie expresses the same thoughts and his view that the teachings of Jesus, the record of the synoptics and the entirety of the New Testament do not support the immortality of the soul. He sees the immortality of the soul as being of Greek philosophical origin and having no basis in divine Scripture.

> A further question arises. Did Jesus lend any support to the idea of the immortality of the soul? The idea of an immortality of the soul as distinct from the resurrection of the body is an essentially Greek idea, expressed for instance, in Plato. This arose partly out of the belief that the body being matter, was evil and therefore mortal. According to this view, all people are essentially immortal in their souls, but not in their bodies. The NT, however, does not support such a sharp dichotomy. There is, in fact, nothing of

---

[25] *Stewart Dingwall Fordyce Salmond, The Christian Doctrine of Immortality. (LaVergne, TN., General Books, 2010), 19 – 20.*
[26] *M.E. Osterhaven, Soul. From Evangelical Dictionary of Theology. Edited by Walter A. Elwell. (Grand Rapids, Baker Books, 1984), 1037.*

relevance on the subject in the synoptics apart from the passages mentioned above, none of which supports it.[27]

HEBREW AND GREEK TERMS FOR SOUL

THE BREATH OF GOD: *NESHAMA*

Examination of the terms used for "breath" and "living being" or "soul" in Genesis 2:7 is revealing. When God breathed into Adam's nostrils the breath of life, the term used for breath is the Hebrew *neshamah*, which returns to God who gave it. Brown, Driver and Briggs define *neshamah* as:

1. *breath of God as hot wind kindling a flame and as a destroying wind.*
2. *breath of man, breath of life; as breathed in by God it is God's breath in man and is characteristic of man,*
3. *every breathing thing, spirit in man.*[28]

Neshamah can be applied to animals such as in Genesis 7:22 when "all in whose nostrils was the breath of the spirit of life, died." However, it may be largely mankind being referred to in that Noatian flood passage. In fact, Victor Hamilton speaks of the uniqueness of mankind's reception of the *neshamah* of God.

> Thus 2:7 may employ the less popular word for breath because it is man, and man alone, who is the recipient of the divine breath. Now divinely formed and inspired, he is a *living person*. Until God breathes into him, man is a lifeless corpse.[29]

Gordon Wenham emphasizes the superiority of mankind over the animal kingdom because man alone is created in God's image. In addition man receives the *neshamah* breath of God personally from the Lord himself.

> Genesis 1:26 – 28 affirms the uniqueness of man by stating that man alone is made in God's image and by giving man authority over the animals. There may be a similar suggestion here, in that man alone receives the breath of God directly (cf. 2:7 and 2:19. Man's authority over the animals is evident in that he is authorized to name them.[30]

---

[27] Donald Guthrie, *New Testament Theology*. (Downers Grove, InterVarsity Press, 1981), 819.
[28] F. Brown, S. Driver, and C. Briggs. *The Brown-Driver-Briggs Hebrew and English Lexicon*. (Peabody, Hendrickson Publishers, 2005), 675.
[29] Victor Hamilton, *The Book Of Genesis, Chapters 1 – 17*. (Grand Rapids, William B. Eerdmans Publishing Company, 1990), 159.

The prophet Job speaks of his life breath as being *neshamah* four times:

Job 27:3 for as long as life is in me, and the breath (*neshamah*) of God is in my nostrils,

32:8 but it is a spirit (ruwach) in man and the breath (neshamah) of the Almighty gives them understanding.

33:4 The Spirit (ruwach) of God has made me, and the breath (neshamah) of the Almighty gives me life.

34:14 - 15 If He should determine to do so, if He should gather to Himself His spirit (*ruwach*) and His breath (*neshamah*), all flesh would perish together, and man would return to dust.

Predominantly in Scripture, *neshamah* is the breath in man while *ruwach* is used in reference to God's Spirit and as the life-giving force in both men and animals.

Speaking of death and the dissolution of the elements of life, Solomon writes:

Ecclesiastes 12:7 Then the dust will return to the earth as it was, and the spirit (ruwach) will return to God who gave it.

Ownership of the spirit in man remains with God who gave it originally in Eden.

The spirit is not ours, nor is it us, in terms of our possession of a soul. Rather, it is God's sole possession. As breathed in by God, it is God's breath in man, not ours. In Ecclesiastes 12 *ruwach* indicates "the spirit of a rational being."

> The process described here is the reversal of Gen. 2:7. The end of life is the dissolution. Humans return to the dust whence they came, while the life-breath given by God returns to its original possessor. This is a picture of dissolution, not of immortality, as if there were a *reditus animae ad Deum,* 'the return of the soul to God.' There is no question of the soul here, but of the life breath, a totally different category of thought.[31]

LIVING BEING OR SOUL: NEPHESH

There is also no question of this breath given to Adam being the Holy Spirit, as in the third person of the Trinity. If this breath given to Adam were

---

[30] *Gordon J. Wenham, Genesis 1 – 15, Word Biblical Commentary. (Waco, Word Books, Publisher, 1987), 61.*
[31] *Roland Murphy, Ecclesiastes. (Dallas, Word Books, 1992), 120.*

the Holy Spirit then the Hebrew in Genesis would read *qodesh ruwach*; Holy Spirit. The breath given to Adam by the Creator, whom we also know as our Lord Jesus Christ, (John 1:1 – 3 & 14, and Colossians 1:16) was Jesus' own breath. The breath, *neshamah*, was definitely not the very person of the Holy Spirit. Jesus' breath, *neshamah*, is also defined as *vital breath, divine inspiration and intellect*.[32] Consequently, our vital breath is more than mere air breathed into Adam's lungs by the Lord, but it also contains something of God's very intellect and divine inspiration. Therefore he made us with a sensibility and desire to peer into and understand the spiritual and divine knowledge and mysteries that only he can impart to a human mind. We are able to comprehend the spiritual because of his very divine, spiritual, intellectual mental capacity, which he has given to mentally and spiritually activate every human being. Only humans have something of the intellect of God dwelling in us. This is not granted as a mental proclivity to the animal kingdom. As a result human beings enjoy life on a far higher spiritual and intellectual plane than any beast ever could. Animals however, are also living beings, Hebrew *nephesh* (Genesis 1:30), just as are human beings. We, and the animals, are all living beings. The only distinct difference between us, being our mental state, capacity and make-up, which for humans includes the spiritual element of divine intellect. George Eldon Ladd makes this point very well.

> The contrast between the Greek and Hebrew views of God and the world is reinforced further by the Old Testament anthropology. Hebrew man is not like the Greek man – a union of soul and body and thus related to two worlds. He is flesh animated by God's breath (*ruach*), who is thus constituted a living soul (*nephesh*) (Gen.2:7; 7:22). *Nephesh* (soul) is not a part of man; it is man himself viewed as a living creature. *Nephesh* is life, both of men (Ex. 21:23; Ps. 33:19) and of animals (Prov. 12:10). If *nephesh* is man as a living creature, it can be used for man himself and indicate man as a person and also become a synonym for 'I,' 'myself.'[33]

It is then the combination of the elements of the earth in union with the divine breath of God, which causes us to be a living being or soul. This is an important concept to understand. We, as living beings or souls, are tied to the physical for our existence. The soul is not some ethereal and metaphysical spirit that lives aside from the body, as in Greek thought.

---

[32] *James Strong, Strong's Exhaustive Concordance of the Bible, Updated Edition. (Peabody, Hendrickson Publishers, Inc., 2007), Dictionary of Hebrew Words, 1543.*
[33] *George Eldon Ladd, The Pattern of New Testament Truth. (Grand Rapids, Wm B. Eerdmans Publishing Co., 1968), 37.*

Body and spirit must be merged in order for the creation of the soul to take place. The soul then is the living product, the end result of the body and the breath of God being absorbed into unity.

> In the Old Testament and the New Testament man is a complete being only as his body and spirit are in union. He is then a living soul or person. While some have understood the Genesis narrative as teaching that man was created immortal and that sin brought mortality, it would seem better to interpret the account as teaching that man would have gained immortality through a period of testing in which he would be obedient to the divine commands. If death was the penalty for sin, life was to be the reward for obedience.[34]

Kaiser sees the creation of man in the same way. He recognizes that the living soul requires both the presence of the material body and the life-giving breath of God. In fact, he sees both man and woman originating from this special combination of material body and the divine breath of God.

> Adam was not 'alive' (*nepes hayyah*, literally, but inaccurately, 'living soul') until God had taken some of the dust of the ground, shaped it, and breathed into it the breath of life. Now to be sure, there are anthropomorphic expressions here, but they are figures of God's direct activity. Man's vitality was a direct gift from God, for prior to that he was not 'alive' – that much is certain!
>
> Eve too was 'built' (*banah*) by God, yet in such a way that her propinquity to Adam was assured. She was to be 'bone of (his) bone and flesh of (his) flesh' (Gen.2:23). Together they originated from the hand of God. Man was so linked to the soil that as his fortunes went, so did the fortunes of nature; and woman was likewise linked to man, for she was 'taken from man.'[35]

THE GREEK *PNEUMA* AND *PSEUCHE*

So far we have explored only the Hebrew derivation of the word "soul" or "living being" and the Scriptural fact that unlike Greek philosophy, Scripture identifies the soul as mortal in that it does not and cannot exist in the absence of the physical body. The Hebrew *nephesh*, a living being, is applied in Scripture to either human beings or to animals.

---

[34] Walter A. Elwell, General Editor. *Evangelical Dictionary of Theology*. (Grand Rapids, Baker Books, 1984), 552.
[35] Walter C. Kaiser, Jr. *Toward An Old Testament Theology*. Grand Rapids, Zondervan Publishing House, 1991), 75.

The Greek equivalent to the Hebrew *nephesh*, for life or soul, is *pseuche*, which is defined as "breath" and has to do with animal life only. On the other hand the Greek *pneuma* is defined as "the rational soul" which obviously applies to human beings alone. Thayer gives five rather comprehensive definitions of *pneuma*:

1. A movement of air.
2. The spirit, the vital principle by which the body is animated.
3. A spirit, a simple essence, possessed of the power of knowing, desiring, deciding, and acting.
4. God's power and agency.
5. The disposition and influence which fills and governs the soul of anyone; the efficient source of any power, affection, emotion, desire, etc.[36]

In Scripture it is apparent that human beings do not possess souls, rather they are souls. I recall a seminary professor opening one of our class sessions in which he made the following statement that seemed to shock some but not me. The statement was, "I want you all to understand one thing in particular today, that is that you do not have a soul, rather you are a soul!" In that statement he conveyed the same understanding of Scripture that is being discovered and promoted in this volume. Though the adherents to this philosophy may constitute a minority in Christianity, nevertheless there does exist a strong minority who have adopted this view. Among them is Norman Geisler. He states the following regarding scientific evidence for Traducianism, which he seems to favor:

> Remembering that *soul* (Heb: *nephesh* and Gk: *pseuche*) means "life," and that a human life is a human soul, the scientific evidence that human life (the soul) begins at conception is strong.[37]

Hodge writes of Olshausen who believed in the unity of body and spirit in forming the soul. "He held that the individuality of man depends on the body; so that without a body there can be no soul."[38]

One leading theological lexicon based on Walter Bauer's word study, gives definitions for both pseuche and pneuma. These definitions can seem confusing and indicate how it is that many exegetes use one or the other in an interchangeable manner.

---

[36] *Joseph H. Thayer, Thayer's Greek-English Lexicon of the New Testament. (Grand Rapids, Baker Book House, 1977), 520 - 523*
[37] *Norman Geisler, Systematic Theology, Volume Three. (Minneapolis, Bethany House, 2004), 34.*
[38] *Charles Hodge, Systematic Theology, Volume III, Soteriology. (Peabody, Hendrickson Publishers, 2003), 732.*

Pseuche: life, soul. It is often impossible to draw hard and fast lines in the use of this multivalent word. Generally it is used in reference to dematerialized existence or being, but, apart from other data, the fact that "pi" is also used as a dog's name suggests that the primary component is not metaphysical. Life on earth in its animating aspect making bodily function possible, breath of life, life-principle, soul, of animals and human beings. The condition of being alive, earthly life, life itself. The seat and center of the inner human life in its many and varied aspects, soul. An entity with personhood, person.

Pneuma: Air in movement, blowing, breathing. Wind. That which animates or gives life to the body, breath. Life-spirit, a breathing entity. A part of human personality, spirit. As the source and seat of insight, feeling, and will, generally as the representative part of human inner life. A person's self or ego. Spiritual state, state of mind, disposition. An independent non-corporeal being, in contrast to a being that can be perceived by the physical senses, spirit. God's being as controlling influence, with focus on association with humans, Spirit. The spirit of life. The Spirit of God as exhibited in the character or activity of God's people or selected agents.[39]

Although the two Greek terms, *pseuche* and *pneuma*, are two entirely different words they are often used interchangeably, and that can create problems in interpretation. Strong gives a more definitive definition. *Pseuche* #5590 is: "breath (has to do with animal life only. Distinguished from #4151 *pneuma*, which is the rational immortal *soul* and #2222, *zoe*, which is mere vitality even in plants)."[40] Strong sees that *pseuche* is a spirit or breathing creature as in any animal life as opposed to *pneuma* being the rational, and in his view, "the immortal soul." It is the "breath" of God, Gk. *pseuche*, which begets the rational soul, Gk. *pneuma*.

N.T. Wright gives support to the term *pseuche* or *psyche* as conveying the idea of physical human life and our state as living beings. This would not include a metaphysical application of the term *psyche* as seen in its usage as *soul*.

We should note as well, in relation to the passage in I Peter and some others, that the word *soul* is rare in this sense in the early

---

[39] *Walter Bauer, A Greek-English Lexicon of the New Testament and other Early Christian Literature, Third Edition. Frederick William Danker, General Editor. (Chicago, The University of Chicago Press, 2000), 832 – 835, 1098 – 1099.*
[40] *James Strong, Strong's Exhaustive Concordance of the Bible. (Peabody, Hendrickson Publishers, Inc., 2007), 1685.*

> Christian writings. The word *psyche* was very common in the ancient world and carried a variety of meanings. Despite its frequency both in later Christianity and (for instance) in Buddhism, the New Testament doesn't use it to describe, so to speak, the bit of you that will ultimately be saved. The word *psyche* seems here to refer, like the Hebrew *nephesh*, not to a disembodied inner part of the human being but to what we might call the person or even the personality. And the point in I Peter 1 (:9) is that this person, the "real you," is *already* being saved and will one day receive that salvation in full bodily form. That is why Peter quite rightly plants the hope for salvation firmly in the resurrection of Jesus. God has, he says, "given us new birth to a living hope by the resurrection of Jesus the Messiah from the dead."[41]

Unfortunately it seems, these two terms, *psyche* and *pneuma*, are used interchangeably in theological reasoning. Such usage is illustrated well in the definition of soul from The Catholic Encyclopedia:

> The soul is the real spiritual substance created by God which, united to the body, constitutes a man. Man is of the "image of God:" the soul is immortal. The soul is declared by the Council of Vienne to be the immediate substantial form of the body.
> ...To understand the soul, it is necessary to look at the person in relation to his capability for sin and redemption. Theologically it is through this recognition of human sinfulness that we arise from the plane of nature to that of grace. The Bible does not recognize the Greek dichotomy of body and soul. The spirit (soul) of the human person is the noblest part; but in the OT the spirit is considered as life itself, that which God breathes into the person and without this the body is dead. Man by himself, a creature of flesh and blood, is a human entity without grace, incapable of achieving his own redemption. This could only come through being born again through Christ and the Holy Spirit.[42]

Broderick freely uses *soul* and *spirit* interchangeably. Even though he does not accept the Greek dichotomy of body and soul, he nevertheless accepts the Greek philosophical position that the soul is the noblest part of the person. He also accepts and promotes the idea that "the soul is immortal."

---

[41] *N.T. Wright, Surprised By Hope. (New York, Harper Collins, 2008), 152.*
[42] *Robert C. Broderick, The Catholic Encyclopedia. (Nashville, Thomas Nelson Inc., Publishers, 1976), 560 – 561.*

It is the assertion of this work that the soul is not immortal nor is it the noblest part of the person but rather that the soul is the entirety of the person. The soul is our life, it is the sum total of the breath of God and the body while in vivified living combination.

Odom helps to clarify this issue and sees the soul as our life, Heb. nephesh. He sees Jesus' quotation of Isaiah 10:18 as a reference to the temporary destruction of the human soul or life until the resurrection and judgment in which the Lord can ultimately destroy the soul eternally.

> In fact, God speaks of the kindling of fire, in the future, which shall consume "both soul [*nephesh*] and body." Isaiah 10:18. That reminds us that Jesus Himself, nearly eight hundred years later, said: "Fear not them which kill the body, but are not able to kill the soul [*pseuche*]: but rather fear him which is able to destroy both soul [*pseuche*] and body in hell." Matthew 10:28. Man may kill a human soul and thereby cause it to be dead temporarily – that is, until the resurrection day, when it shall live again. (In Greek, the language in which the New Testament was written, the word *pseuche* corresponds to the Hebrew term *nephesh*.)[43]

According to Geisler, the concept of the immortal pre-existence of the soul comes down to us from Plato. Platonic philosophy "asserts that all souls existed before the world began - they are eternal and uncreated."[44] The Cambridge Dictionary of Philosophy gives additional insight regarding the origin of Plato's philosophy on the soul.

> Soul, also called spirit, an entity supposed to be present only in living things, corresponding to the Greek *psyche* and Latin *anima*. Since there seems to be no material difference between an organism in the last moments of its life and the organism's newly dead body, many philosophers since the time of Plato have claimed that the soul is an immaterial component of an organism. Because only material things are observed to be subject to dissolution. Plato took the soul's immateriality as grounds for its immortality. [45]

Plato's pagan position is diametrically opposite to the teaching of Scripture in that the soul did not have a pre-existent eternity but rather that the soul was the life of Adam, created by God at Genesis 2:7. Adam's soul,

---

[43] *Robert Leo Odom, Is Your Soul Immortal? Ukiah, CA., Orion Publishing, 2007), 26 – 27.*
[44] *Norman Geisler, Systematic Theology, Volume Three. (Minneapolis, Bethany House, 2004), 32.*
[45] *Robert Audi, General Editor. The Cambridge Dictionary Of Philosophy, Second Edition. (Cambridge, Cambridge University Press, 1999), 866.*

or life, had no pre-existence and no immortality. Adam's life, or soul, was subject to death.

Kaiser also adds to the biblical view by stating the obvious that Adam was not alive until God took of the dust of the ground, forming it into the body, the corpse of Adam, and then through the transforming process of breathing the breath of life into Adam's nostrils. "Man's vitality was a direct gift from God, for prior to that he was not 'alive' that much is certain!"[46]

Buddhist theology has a sense of life continuing beyond one's physical death. This continuation of life is accomplished through the continual rebirth of the soul into other lives or other forms of life. In Buddhism a major factor in the need for reincarnation is the problem of desire, which creates the disease called *dukkha*. Though the world and personal identity are largely illusory, the desire for the attractions of the world create the disease and in turn there is created an ongoing necessity to be reborn until all desire for such pleasures and attachments are dispelled and the soul is filled with more *karma*, or the achievement of perfection.[47]

Hindu philosophy sees reincarnation as simply a natural part of the cycle of life. In this cycle the soul is immortal, it was not created nor will it ever die. Ormerod confirms this view regarding the continual cycle of life.

> For the Hindu believer, reincarnation is part of the great cycle of life, in which the soul is reborn again and again, as it moves along the path of perfection, until it reaches union with God and achieves a cosmic consciousness.[48]

Edward Fudge is perhaps the premier contemporary theological advocate in the promotion of Conditionalism regarding the mortality of the soul. He speaks of the biblical position that the soul of man was created in Eden and that man is dependent upon God for creation, life, sustenance as well as everlasting life. He asserts that neither Plato nor his student-successor Socrates saw the soul and the human life found in the body in the same way that writers of the Old Testament Scriptures did.[49] The Old Testament reveals that the soul came into existence at the moment of the creation of Adam and that it was the product of the material corpse being invigorated by the very breath, *neshamah*, of God. That divine breath was composed of not merely air, but also was permeated with something of the divine intellect

---

[46] *Walter C. Kaiser, Jr., Toward an Old Testament Theology. (Grand Rapids, Zondervan Publishing House, 1991), 75.*

[47] *Neil Ormerod, Creation, Grace, and Redemption. (Maryknoll, Orbis Books, 2007), 43.*

[48] *Ibid, 193.*

[49] *Edward William Fudge and Robert A. Peterson, Two Views of Hell. (Downers Grove, Inter Varsity Press, 2000), 22.*

of God. The soul, *nephesh*, a living being, is mere animal life, according to Scripture, and is applied in Genesis not only to man as a "living soul" (KJV), or as a "living being" (NAS) but also in Genesis 1:20 & 24 the term *hay nephesh* is applied to the sea creatures and the beasts of the earth.

On the one hand, if man is a mortal soul, with a limited duration, then so are animals of limited lifetime. Alternately, if the soul is eternal and immortal then animals also have eternal immortal souls as well as mankind. This is obviously a preposterous idea and yet it is a natural extension of Genesis 2 to all members of the living animal kingdom if *nephesh* indicates soul in the sense of an immortal life. Certainly *nephesh* does not actually indicate anything akin to Hindu and Greek philosophy regarding the immortality of the soul. The Bible makes it obvious that the soul, animal life, is a temporary and mortal condition.

> According to Plato, each human being has a body that is mortal and will finally die. Plato taught that each person also has a soul that is immortal and cannot die. Plato's student Socrates continued his master's philosophy. As he faced his own execution, Socrates welcomed death, for to him it meant escaping the lower realm of mortal bodies and returning to the higher sphere of immortal souls. Like his teacher Plato, Socrates believed that the soul cannot die nor cease to exist. Plato died before Jesus was born, and thus before Jesus revealed that God *'can destroy both soul and body in hell'* (Mt 10:28). Socrates' view also differs from the view expressed by his predecessors, the Old Testament writers, who consistently dreaded death as the end of life. Unlike those Scriptures, Socrates did not view man in relation to the living God.
>
> …The Old Testament writers disagree with later Greek philosophers who portray humans as immortal souls entrapped for a time in mortal bodies.[50]

The Apostle Paul's theology regarding the coming resurrection of the faithful dead was the theology of the first century church. Paul expresses it fully in I Corinthians 15:50 – 58 and in I Thessalonians 4:13 – 18. In both places he emphasizes the coming resurrection of those who sleep in Christ. He speaks also of the fact that at the resurrection the "mortal must put on immortality."

---

[50] *Edward William Fudge and Robert A. Peterson, Two Views of Hell. (Downers Grove, Inter Varsity Press, 2000), 22.*

> I Corinthians 15:51 – 54 Behold, I tell you a mystery; we will not all sleep, but we will all be changed, in a moment, in the twinkling of an eye, at the last trumpet; for the trumpet will sound, and the dead will be raised imperishable, and we will be changed. For this perishable must put on the imperishable, and this mortal must put on immortality. But when this perishable will have put on the imperishable, and this mortal will have put on immortality, then will come about the saying that is written, 'Death is swallowed up in victory.'

Paul is not the only New Testament writer who focuses on the resurrection from the dead. John demonstrates in Scripture that believers will experience resurrection from the dead. He also indicates that those who have accepted Jesus as Savior in this age are the ones who will be ordained as kings and priests with Christ and will have an initial reign with him for a thousand years. In Revelation 22:5 John extends that reign and rule to "forever."

> Revelation 20:6 Blessed and holy is the one who has a part in the first resurrection; over these the second death has no power, but they will be priests of God and of Christ and will reign with Him for a thousand years.

We must then ask some common sense questions. If believers are already in heaven, according to traditional Christian theology, enjoying a beatific vision and the pleasures of paradise, why is a resurrection of the dead from the grave necessary at the return of Christ? Have we forgotten the rather plain and simple words of Jesus who told Nicodemus in John 3:13 that "no one has ascended into heaven, but he who descended from heaven: the son of man."

Traditional Christian teaching on the state of the soul and the state of the dead produces some rather contradictory notions. Odom relates an experience of his with a traveling evangelist who pitched a tent in his city to conduct a campaign. Odom assisted him in setting up his tent which gave him opportunity to discuss the important matter of the state of the dead and the resurrection. When Odom asked the evangelist about what happens to the righteous and the wicked at death, the preacher stated the obvious of the traditional view that upon death the righteous believer would go immediately to heaven and begin the process of enjoying eternal bliss while the impenitent unbeliever would go immediately to hell and suffer the torments of eternal hellfire at the expiration of this life.

Upon further questioning by Odom regarding the second coming and the future judgment, the preacher sought to clarify its purpose. He indicated that God would reward the righteous with everlasting life and would punish the wicked with eternal suffering and that these rewards and punishments would be meted out at the general judgment after the second Advent.

Odom was puzzled by the manner and sequence of these events. He then went on to make a quizzical statement and question.

> Then I remarked: "That puzzles me. A few minutes ago you told me that your church teaches that immediately after he dies a wicked person goes down into hell fire to be eternally punished by torment; and that at death a righteous person is taken immediately up to heaven to dwell there eternally in joy and happiness. Do you mean that the impenitent sinner is to be judged and punished *twice* – that is, that at death he will be judged and immediately sent to suffer torment in hell fire for the sins that he has committed, and that later, at the second advent of Christ, he will be resurrected, judged, and condemned *again* to eternal torment in the fires of hell for those same sins? Will Jesus at His second coming have all the wicked called up from the lake of fire to enter their graves to be resurrected, to be judged, and to be sent into hell fire a *second time*? Will the redeemed then be called down from heaven to enter their graves, to be resurrected, to be judged, and to be taken to heaven a *second time*?"
>
> I shall never forget the puzzled expression that came over that preacher's face. He honestly replied: "I have never thought about that!" And, scratching the top of his head with one hand, and gesturing with the other, he added: "I am going to write to some of the big men in our church to find out what they have to say about that!"[51]

Sometimes traditional Christian teaching makes this writer scratch his head too.

How about you?

---

[51] *Robert Leo Odom, Is Your Soul Immortal? (Ukiah, CA., Orion Publishing, 2007), 18.*

Only God Is Immortal

In chapter five we will deal with the supposed ascensions to heaven by Enoch, Elijah and the thief on the cross. The obvious inference of Scripture is that our lives, our souls, are not immortal. On the contrary, man is mortal and the only one admitted in Scripture to be immortal is God. He alone has no beginning and no end in his divine and eternal immortality.

> The word "immortal" is used but once in the Bible, where it speaks of the Deity as "the King eternal, immortal, invisible, the only wise God." 1 Timothy 1:17. [52]

I Timothy 6:16 speaks of Christ Jesus, a member of the Triune God-head, "who alone possesses immortality." This statement by Paul demonstrates the wide gulf that separates the life and nature of mortal man in relation to the incomparably immortal ever-living Godhead.

Josef Pieper illustrates how the New Testament applies the term "immortality" only to Jesus Christ. In addition he demonstrates that Thomas Aquinas only referred to man as being immortal in association with the resurrected believers and their paradisiacal existence.

> The New Testament does not once mention the "immortal soul"; the word "immortality" itself occurs only three times, and then the immortality is attributed not to the soul, but to the risen Christ and the – again bodily – man of the coming eon. What is more, the phrase "immortality of the soul" is strikingly absent from the great theological tradition. Thomas Aquinas, for example, normally does not call the soul "immortal"; he speaks, rather, of its imperishability and incorruptibility. If he does chance to mention "immortality" in connection with man, he has in mind only paradisiacal man or the man of the New Eon who has been resurrected from the dead.[53]

Even in medieval times, when the doctrine of the immortality of the soul had been well entrenched in prevailing Christian doctrine, some still believed in the necessity of a bodily resurrection. This is born out in the writings of Thomas and Bernard.

> Mainstream medieval theologians like Thomas and Bernard insisted on the bodily resurrection. They, like the New Testament and early church fathers, held a strong view of God's good creation. They knew that it must be reaffirmed, not abandoned. But a good deal of Western Medieval piety then took a very

---

[52] *Robert Leo Odom, Is Your Soul Immortal? (Ukiah, CA., Orion Publishing, 2007), 57*
[53] *Josef Pieper, Death and Immortality. (South Bend, St. Augustine's Press, 2000), 29.*

different turn, in which the twin destinations of heaven and hell and the possible intermediate destination of purgatory became far more important and in which the language of resurrection, insofar as it was retained at all, seemed simply to be a rather special way of talking about heaven, which was the primary category. This has had all kinds of unfortunate results, to which we shall come in a moment. [54]

This study is convincing me more fully than ever before that the elements of mainstream theology, which are based on traditional Christian teaching, are in many cases crumbling before my eyes under the powerful hammer of Scripture and the re-examination of pagan philosophical views. Those pagan philosophies have been incorporated into Christian doctrine over time. The Bible does not support the doctrine of man's possession of an immortal soul nor does it support current active life in heaven for those believers who have passed from this temporal life.

Ray Anderson also supports this view. Likewise he demonstrates that the Old Testament does not encourage the idea of the immortality of the soul but rather shows that the soul and body are both mortal and consequently subject to death

> The concept of the immortality of the soul, or of the immortality of the human self as a natural state, is not a concept that finds support in the Bible…
>
> The belief that human persons possess an immortal soul, however, runs contrary to the Hebrew anthropology which, as we have seen, defines the soul and body as both subject to death. There is no concept of an immortal soul in Hebrew anthropology as presented in the Old Testament. The New Testament does not once mention the 'immortal soul;' the word 'immortal' occurs only three times, and then the immortality is not attributed to the soul but to the risen Christ and the embodied person in the new age (cf. 1 Corinthians 15:53ff; 1 Timothy 6:16).[55]

PLATO

Oscar Cullman reproved the theologians of the 1950's who held to the Platonic Greek view of the immortality of the soul. In doing so they were neglecting the clear teaching of Scripture regarding the resurrection of those who in their mortal lives succumbed to death. He saw that Scripture has been abrogated in favor of Greek fables.

---

[54] N.T. Wright, *Surprised by Hope*. (New York, Harper Collins, 2008), 158.
[55] Ray S. Anderson, *Theology, Death And Dying*. (New York, Basil Blackwell Inc., 1986), 57.

> The fact that later Christianity effected a link between the two beliefs and that today the ordinary Christian simply confuses them has not persuaded me to be silent about what I, in common with most exegetes, regard as true; and all the more so, since the link established between the expectation of the 'resurrection of the dead' and the belief in 'the immortality of the soul' is not in fact a link at all but renunciation of one in favour of the other. I Corinthians 15 has been sacrificed for the *Phaedo*.[56]

This matter of the soul being immortal is completely unbiblical and without genuine support in Scripture. N.T. Wright weighs in with those who do not see heaven as the destiny of the saved. He does not see the saved as anything but mortal in their current existence.

> Second, do we have immortal souls, and if so, what are they? Again, much Christian and sub-Christian tradition has assumed that we all do indeed have souls that need saving and that the soul, if saved, will be the part of us that goes to heaven when we die. All this, however, finds minimal support in the New Testament, including the teaching of Jesus, where the word *soul* though rare, reflects when it does occur underlying Hebrew or Aramaic words referring not to a disembodied entity hidden within the outer shell of the disposable body but rather to what we would call the whole person or personality, seen as being confronted by God. As to immortality, I Timothy 6:16 declares that only God himself has immortality, and 2 Timothy 1:10 declares that immortality has only come to light, and hence is presumably only available, through the gospel. In other words, the idea that every human possesses an immortal soul, which is the "real" part of them, finds little support in the Bible.[57]

Plato and Scripture are not compatible. How long will it be before the Bible becomes the standard for Christian doctrine and the *Phaedo* is placed back on the bookshelf of forgotten uninspired pagan religions?

Frank Thielman writes about the significance of the body and soul in ancient Greco-Roman anthropology. He cites a passage from the Roman Cicero who actually seemed to be promoting modern day Mortalism in one of the views he presented.

> In Greco-Roman society the belief was common that death released the soul from the shackles of the body. Cicero, writing in the Latin West in the first century B.C., ridicules belief in the

---

[56] Oscar Cullmann, *Immortality of the Soul or Resurrection of the Dead? (London, The Epworth Press, 1958), 7 – 8.*
[57] *N.T. Wright, Surprised By Hope. (New York, Harper Collins, 2008), 28.*

elaborate Greek mythology of the underworld – descent at death to a cavity in the earth where souls must cross Lake Acheron, pass by the fierce three-headed dog Cerberus, and stand before the judges Minos and Rhadamanthus. He then discusses the other more sensible options:

> Some consider death the separation of the soul from the body; some think there is no such separation, but that soul and body perish together and the soul is annihilated with the body. Of those who think that there is a separation of the soul some hold that it is at once dispersed in space, others that it survives a long time, others that it survives forever.[58]

AUGUSTINE

Augustine of Hippo was perhaps the greatest theologian of early Christianity. His influence is strongly felt today in the established doctrinal positions of the Christian Church. He was born in 354 AD in Tagaste, North Africa, to a pagan father, Patricius, and to a Christian mother named Monica. Early in his career he was an adherent of the teachings of Mani who founded the Manichaean heresy, which involved a complex Gnostic system, that promised salvation by reception of knowledge. He later forsook it with a number of treatises written in opposition to that religion. Manichaeism incorporated certain aspects of the Buddhist, Christian and Persian religions. While teaching in Milan he studied neo-platonic philosophy and the sermons of Ambrose. He was baptized by Ambrose in 387 AD and returned to live with his mother until her death shortly thereafter.[59]

Even in speaking of her death, Augustine betrays his platonic views. He believed that her soul was released from imprisonment in the body at the point of her death.

> And so on the ninth day of her illness, when she was fifty-six and I was thirty-three, her pious and devoted soul was set free from the body.[60]

Augustine's pagan father, the Christian influence of his mother, the teachings of Ambrose and his study of neo-platonism brought about a somewhat confused and synchristic view of Christianity which expressed itself in his teachings on man and his soul. It is inescapable in his works to

---

[58] *Frank Thielman, Theology of the New Testament. (Grand Rapids, Zondervan, 2005), 301.*
[59] *Walter A. Elwell, General Editor. Evangelical Dictionary of Theology. Grand Rapids, Baker Book House, 1997), 105.*
[60] *Saint Augustine, Confessions. Translated by R.S. Pine-Coffin. (London, Penguin Books Group, 1961), 200.*

see that he accepted the Hellenistic platonic doctrine of the immortality of the soul.

Augustine believed in and accepted the notion of the immortality of the soul. In his writings he agreed with Porphyry's correction of platonic teaching regarding souls re-inhabiting another body after the death of the previous being. It was Plato's view that immortal souls could and would migrate from one being to another without difficulty. Porphyry, and Augustine, as evidenced by his agreement, believed that the souls of men would only re-inhabit another human being.

> If it is considered improper to correct Plato on any point, why did Porphyry himself offer a number of important corrections? For it is an established fact that Plato wrote that after death the souls of men return to earth, and even enter into the bodies of beasts. The same belief was held also by Plotinus, the teacher of Porphyry. Nevertheless, Porphyry refused to accept it, quite rightly. His theory was that human souls return, but into men's bodies, not the bodies which they have left, but into others, into new bodies.[61]

In regards to eternity, Augustine also cites Porphyry as having the correct view as opposed to that of Plato. In his taking Porphyry's side, he also reveals his own perspective of the state of immortality as regards the soul. The Platonists see that nothing can have an eternal future without already having had an eternal past. Yet Augustine sides with Porphyry in accepting that the soul had a time of initial creation but that it also does have an eternal future.

> Since these are questions which are beyond the competence of human wit to sift to the bottom, why do we not trust instead in the divine power which tells us that the soul itself is, like other things, created out of non-existence? The Platonists are evidently satisfied with justifying their refusal to believe this by the argument that nothing can have an eternal future which has not had an eternal past. And yet, when treating of the universe, and the gods which, he says, God has created in the universe, Plato distinctly affirms that they come into being and have a beginning; yet he declares that they will not have an end, but will continue for ever, thanks to the mighty will of their creator.[62]

Augustine's belief regarding the soul incorporated a view that, in spite of the fact that the soul is immortal, it can also be brought to a state of

---

[61] *Saint Augustine, City of God, Translated by Henry Bettenson. (London, Penguin Books Group, 2003), 417.*
[62] *Ibid. 419-420.*

existence to a lesser degree of life. To him, the soul never ceases to exist and feel, even if only in the slightest level, even though the body itself can be completely devoid of life.

> The soul therefore derives life from God, when its life is good – for its life cannot be good except when God is active in it to produce what is good – while the body derives life from the soul when the soul is alive in the body, whether the soul derives its life from God or not. For the life of the bodies of the ungodly is not the life of their souls but of their bodies, a life which souls can confer even when those souls are dead, that is, when God abandons them; for their own life, in virtue of which they are immortal, still persists, in however low a degree.[63]

The Scriptural second death was, to Augustine, the worse of all possible situations for the body and the soul. He saw therein a hopeless condition of eternal suffering for both of those elements, body and soul, in continued union for eternity.

> Nevertheless with the help of the grace of our Redeemer we may be enabled to decline (or avoid) that second death. For that death, which means not the separation of soul from body but the union of both for eternal punishment, is the more grievous death; it is the worst of all evils. There, by contrast, men will not be in the situations of 'before death' and 'after death', but always 'in death', and for this reason they will never be living, never dead, but dying for all eternity.[64]

Clark Pinnock understands that a major reason for the continuing promotion of the idea that the soul is immortal and that it is destined for either heaven or hell upon death is that such a concept can be used to keep people in fear and thus under the influence of traditional doctrinal teaching and church leadership. The immortality of the soul and the potential eternal suffering in hell can be used as a whip to keep people in line with their views.

> One can distinguish at least three such influences on the traditional side from experience and culture. First, there is the Hellenistic belief in the immortality of the soul. As Swinburne says, "I suspect that one factor which influenced the Fathers and scholastics to affirm eternal sensatory punishment was their belief in the natural immortality of the soul." Here is a secular belief influencing theology. Second, it has been common to use hell as

---

[63] *Saint Augustine, City of God. Translated by Henry Bettenson. (London, Penguin Books Group, 2003), 52.*
[64] *Ibid, 521.*

a moral deterrent. Pusey used the belief as a whip to keep people in line, and he was not alone in this. The orthodox often fear what will happen in society if the belief in everlasting torment were to decline. Would people not behave without moral restraint and the society devolve into anarchy? For such reasons William Shedd considered no doctrine more important than hell, given the increase of wealth and sinful excess he saw then, involves a strongly contextual factor. Third, Jonathan Edwards used hell to frighten people into faith, and he is not alone in this either. I have heard people oppose hell as annihilation on the grounds that it isn't frightening enough and would let the wicked off too easily. Everlasting conscious punishment is a huge stick that some people do not want to give up. It has always been used to promote the urgency of missions, and the strongest objection to any revision may well come from missionary agencies.[65]

Augustine attempted to explain the creation of man in terms of body and soul. He seems to have ignored the Scripture at Genesis 2:7 that the formation of Adam was of two elements, the dust of the ground, and the breath of God. Those two elements, in combination, created the soul or life of Adam. There is no soul without the breath of God or without the body. Here Augustine betrays his platonic perspective of body and soul.

> But they say, he already had a soul. Otherwise, he would not have been called a man, since man is not merely a body or merely a soul, but a being constituted by body and soul together. This is indeed true, for the soul is not the whole man; it is the better part of man, and the body is not the whole man; it is the lower part of him. It is the conjunction of the two parts that is entitled to the name of 'man'; and yet those parts taken separately are not deprived of the appellation even when we speak of them by themselves.[66]

In Augustine's quest for happiness he also speaks of God giving life to his soul. But in his Hellenistic bias he sees that his soul gives life to his body rather than the breath of God infusing life into the body and thus creating the soul or life of man.

> How, then, do I look for you, O Lord? For when I look for you, who are my God, I am looking for a life of blessed happiness. I shall look for you, so that my soul may live. For it is my soul that

---

[65] Clark H. Pinnock, *Four Views Of Hell*. William Crockett, General Editor. (Grand Rapids, Zondervan 1996), 163 – 164.
[66] Saint Augustine, *City of God*. Translated by Henry Bettenson. (London, Penguin Books Group, 2003), 541.

gives life to my body, and it is you who give life to my soul.[67]

The neo-platonic bias of Augustine allows him to then see man as body, mind and soul as separate individual entities. Norman Geisler quotes him saying as much.

> If, again, we were so to define man as to say, Man is a rational substance consisting of mind and body, then without doubt man has a soul that is not body, and a body that is not soul (OT, 15.7) [68]

But this position is wholly platonic and does not square with the teaching of Scripture. In the Bible we do not see Greek dualism. The Greek philosophers saw man as consisting of only two parts. This dualistic view saw man as consisting of a body and of a soul. The body was temporal with a limited existence and was basically evil. On the other hand, man's soul was eternal and was primarily good in its essence.

Scripture teaches no such thing. In the creation story, everything God created in the world was good, including the life, the soul of man, which did not exist outside or without the body, which also was "very good."

> Genesis 1:31 God saw all that he had made, and behold, it was very good. And there was evening and there was morning, the sixth day.

The Bible does not teach that the body is evil. The Bible neither teaches that the soul is immortal nor that it passes from one life or life form to another in any continuing cycle of the immortal soul. In Pauline theology, which comprises the majority of the New Testament books, Paul sees the body as vital for the life of the soul.

> It is un-Pauline to say that I am a soul or spirit living in a body, or that I am a spirit and I have a body; I am body as well as soul or spirit. This is why for Paul the destiny of man requires the resurrection of the body, for human existence by definition is bodily existence.[69]

PAUL ON THE STATE OF THE DEAD

Paul may express his desire "to be absent from the body and to be at home with the Lord" (2 Corinthians 5:8) but at the same time we must

---

[67] *Saint Augustine, Confessions. Translated by R. S. Pine-Coffin. (London, Penguin Books Group, 1961), 226.*
[68] *Norman Geisler, Systematic Theology, Volume Three, Sin Salvation. (Minneapolis, Bethany House, 2004), 71.*
[69] *George Eldon Ladd, The Pattern of New Testament Truth. (Grand Rapids, Wm. B. Eerdmans Publishing Co., 1968), 103.*

understand that Paul accepted the concept of the dead being "asleep" (an O.T. concept) and he presents the theology of Christians coming to life and immortality only at the time of the first resurrection.

> I Thessalonians 4:13 – 18 But we do not want you to be uninformed, brethren, about those who are asleep, so that you will not grieve as do the rest who have no hope. For if we believe that Jesus died and rose again, even so God will bring with Him those who have fallen asleep in Jesus. For this we say to you by the word of the Lord, that we who are alive and remain until the coming of the Lord, will not precede those who have fallen asleep. For the Lord Himself will descend from heaven with a shout, with the voice of the archangel and with the trumpet of God, and the dead in Christ will rise first. Then we who are alive and remain will be caught up together with them in the clouds to meet the Lord in the air, and so we shall always be with the Lord. Therefore comfort one another with these words.

There is no depiction in Paul's writings of Christians going to heavenly bliss upon death. The Old Testament acknowledges that only their spirit, *neshamah*, returns to God who gave it and in the New Testament those spirits remain figuratively under the altar of God in heaven in Revelation 6:9. Speaking of the process of death, Solomon writes:

> Ecclesiastes 12:7 then the dust will return to the earth as it was, and the spirit will return to God who gave it.

Ecclesiastes 3:19 – 21 also focuses on the complete dissolution of the body and the spirit. N.T. Wright formulates his view of this concept of how man's life is only temporary and mortal and that there is no immortality to his existence as a soul.

> Death means that the body returns to the dust, and the breath to God who gave it; meaning not that an immortal part of the person goes to live with God, but that the God who breathed life's breath into human nostrils in the first place will simply withdraw it into his own possession.[70]

The soul consists of body and spirit as stated in Genesis 2:7. These two elements in combination create a life or soul. If the spirit absents the body then there is no longer a life or soul. We see in Ecclesiastes 12:7 that Solomon clarifies the notion that the spirit which gives life returns to God at death, the time of the dissolution of life.

---

[70] N.T. Wright, *The Resurrection Of The Son Of God*. (Minneapolis, Fortress Press, 2003), 98–99.

George Eldon Ladd brings clarity to the matter. He recognizes that it is the resurrection that holds out the hope of our eternal life, not existence in heaven upon death.

> But if our true home is in heaven, this does not mean that the disembodied redeemed soul flies away to heaven there to abide in glory; it means that Christ will come from heaven to earth bringing with him the heavenly life, transforming our lowly mortal bodies of flesh and blood to conform to his glorious body; and this transformation does not occur at death when the soul departs to be with Christ; it occurs at the day of the Lord when "God will bring with him those who have fallen asleep.[71]

It is apparent in this passage that Ladd accepts heaven as our ultimate home and that he accepts the "soul" as a separate metaphysical entity rather than the Scriptural spirit (psyche) returning to heaven at death. However, he does see the concept that the life of a Christian is restored in glorified bodily form at the second coming resurrection. Heaven is not our ultimate home. Revelation shows our ultimate home to be the New Earth and the New Jerusalem, our permanent dwelling place, and the site of God's temple and eternal dwelling, which comes out of heaven to earth (Revelation 21:1 – 2). In the end the Bible pictures heaven coming to earth rather than our going to heaven, which is a crucial reversal of customary Christian teaching.

The Hellenistic philosophy of Augustine has had far-reaching and negative influence on Christian theology. Through Augustine and others who held his views, even the reformers were negatively affected by the view of the immortality of the soul. One principle case is that of John Calvin. Calvin accepted the immortality of the soul and we see that fact in his writings in his *Institutes of the Christian Religion*.

> Moreover, there can be no question that man consists of a body and a soul; meaning by soul, an immortal though created essence, which is his nobler part. Sometimes he is called a spirit. But though the two terms, while they are used together differ in their meaning, still when spirit is used by itself it is equivalent to soul, as when Solomon speaking of death says, that the spirit returns to God who gave it (Eccl 12:7).[72]

According to what has been presented thus far in this work, we can note that Calvin adopts the Greek platonic philosophy of the dualistic nature of the human being. Man consisting of a body and a soul. He also accepts the

---

[71] *George Eldon Ladd, The Pattern of New Testament Truth. (Grand Rapids, Wm. B. Eerdmans Publishing Co., 1968), 107.*
[72] *John Calvin, Institutes of the Christian Religion. Translated by Henry Beveridge. (Peabody, Hendrickson Publishers, 2008), 104 – 105.*

Greek view of the immortality of the soul. He accepts the nobility of the soul as compared to the inferiority of the body. He has a forced view of Solomon's usage of "spirit," Hebrew "ruwach," from Ecclesiastes 12:7. "Ruwach" is defined as "wind, breath, spirit of a rational being." Both the NAS as well as the King James, as opposed to Calvin, get it right. "Ruwach" is spirit rather than "soul."

Unfortunately, the influence of Augustine, Calvin and other major theological voices, won the battles of Church tradition and dogma. Today, Christianity suffers deeply for having a twisted view of the matter of the soul, the matter of salvation, and the matter of blessedness or punishment based on unchristian pagan views brought into our doctrinal professions.

In this chapter we see that the soul was developed at the creation of Adam and Eve. The Bible does not promote the idea of an immortal soul from creation. On the other hand, the Bible does teach that believers will become immortal at the eschatological second coming of Jesus and the resurrection of the faithful.

In Hebrew the living being or soul is *nephesh*, and the term is applied not only to human beings but also to animals, which are living breathing creatures. If *neshamah* indicated immortal life or soul in humans, then the same would have to apply to animals in that they too would have immortal souls in that case. This is a biblically preposterous idea and is certainly not implied by Scripture. A *nephesh*, living being or soul, is simply the designation of a fleshly living being.

In contrast to Greek and pagan philosophy, the biblical view of the soul is one of temporary life, which has the potential of becoming immortal at the resurrection. The soul, at this moment, has nothing immortal about it. We are merely mortal beings who die and our only hope of eternal life is in the gracious hands of God and his merciful judgment.

We have also come to recognize that the influence of Saint Augustine on the church has been strong and effective in bringing a neo-platonic perspective into Christian doctrine. His advocacy of the immortality of the soul has been so deep and powerfully effective that even the reformers accepted his theology.

It is also evident that his views and teachings have brought much harm to Christianity and to Christians as the church has adopted pagan philosophy and non-biblical views in virtually all areas of doctrine. It does matter what the foundational teachings of our faith are. It does matter what their basis is. If their basis is not purely Scriptural, we are watering down and modifying, in a negative sense, the intended understanding and revealed teaching of the word of God. Our understanding of salvation and the salvation of the whole world is at stake in regards to how we view the soul and its nature.

In summary, according to Scripture, the soul is composed of two elements, the physical corpse which is infiltrated with the breath of God. The soul is not metaphysical as it is to the Greeks, rather it is mortal and is only enlivened by the mental capability and breath of God himself. We discovered in this chapter that the Hebrew nephesh is the word for "soul" in the Old Testament, which has its equivalance in the Greek *pneuma* in the New Testament. Both words can be defined as "life" and "living being." Immortality in Scripture is assigned to God only in I Timothy 6:16. No human being is immortal at this moment nor will be except for believers only at the second coming of Christ (I Corinthians 15:50 – 54). We have also seen in this chapter how platonic Hellenistic views infiltrated Christianity in the first few centuries after its inception regarding a belief in the immortality of the soul. Augustine was one of those who came from a pagan background who brought his considerable influence to bear on the subject during his day by incorporating into his theological views the pagan Greek doctrine of the immortality of the soul.

Whether one is a Conditionalist or if one sees a more limited salvation opportunity in this life only, the matter of the soul's mortality or immortality is of great consequence regarding which doctrinal position we choose to espouse. In Chapter four I will explore the Scriptural position regarding the fate of the soul in the final judgment. Annihilation is possible if the soul is mortal. On the other hand eternal suffering and separation from God is inevitable for wicked unbelievers if the soul is immortal.

Chapter Four
Annihilationism In Scripture

CHAPTER FOUR

ANNIHILATIONISM IN SCRIPTURE

Any weeping, wailing, or gnashing of teeth
refers to the grief over receiving one's sentence,
not some ongoing, agonized state of consciousness. [73]

Having dealt with the mortality or immortality of the soul in chapter three we now can discover the possibility of the annihilation of the soul for those who will maintain adamantly a position of lawlessness and unbelief.

Benjamin Warfield wrote of Annihilationism and carefully defined three theories as to how non-believing human beings will be put out of existence. These theories touch on both mortality and immortality as associated with human life.

> Annihilationism: A term designating broadly a large body of theories which unite in contending that human beings pass, or are put, out of existence altogether. These theories fall logically into three classes, according as they hold that all souls, being mortal, actually cease to exist at death; or that, souls being naturally mortal, only those persist in life to which immortality is given by God; or that, though souls are naturally immortal and persist in existence unless destroyed by a force working upon them from without, wicked souls are actually thus destroyed. These three classes of theories may be conveniently called respectively, (1) pure mortalism, (2) conditional immortality, and (3) annihilationism proper. [74]

THE LORD OUR GOD IS A CONSUMING FIRE

In furtherance of the biblical view of Conditionalism it is important to understand that there will come a day when the unrepentant wicked will indeed face the annihilating fire of God. This book does not advocate that there is never going to be a destructive fire, normally referred to as hell. That "lake of fire" will indeed exist at the time of general judgment and the stubbornly unrepentant wicked will meet their end in that terrible and utter destruction known as the second death. In Scripture we find that God is often illustrated as a flame of fire. This flame consists of all-consuming

---

[73] Bradley Jersak, *Her Gates Will Never Be Shut.* (Eugene, WIPF & Stock, 2009), 4.
[74] Benjamin B. Warfield, *The Works of Benjamin B. Warfield, Volume IX, Studies in Theology.* (Grand Rapids, Baker Books, 2003), 447.

and irresistible energy. We see a number of such appearances of the presence of God in Scripture depicting him as a powerful and consuming flame.

In the book of Deuteronomy Moses restated to Israel the law of Mount Sinai. He also recalled to the nation, based on his experience with the Lord, that the God they served was all-powerful and was not to be trifled with or disrespected by their practice of idolatry. Moses had experienced God's power at the episodes of the burning bush; in the pillar of fire and cloud in the wilderness; Mount Sinai being all aflame with the presence of the Lord and also his witness of the presence of the Lord in the heavenly fire which consumed the sacrificial offering placed on the altar of worship at the inauguration of the tabernacle. Moses warned his people against disobedience to the Lord for a very evident reason.

> Deuteronomy 4:24 for the Lord your God is a consuming fire, a jealous God.

Not only do we see this description of God himself in the Old Testament context but the writer of Hebrews in the New Testament repeats the same words in quotation of Deuteronomy 4:24. Thus the thought is confirmed in Scripture by a double reference and double witness to the fact of God's powerful consumptive ability regarding those who refuse him.

Hebrews 12:29 for our God is a consuming fire.

The Lord was and is jealous of the affections of his people. Moses had witnessed the deaths of those who took lightly the word of God when it came to the manner in which he was to be worshipped in the tabernacle and later in the temple. To serve God as one of his appointed priests was a serious matter that needed to be attended to in all sobriety and holiness.

In Leviticus 9 we see how God intervened in the process of inaugurating worship at the dedication of the newly built portable place of worship known as the tabernacle. He had given particular directions as to how the worship system was to be conducted in the previous chapters including the regulations regarding the duties and comportment of the priests. The Lord made certain that the flame of the sacrificial altar would not be just any ordinary fire. He sent the fire to be used in the system and it was the sacred duty of the priests to keep that special heavenly fire alive perpetually.

> Leviticus 9:22 – 24 Then Aaron lifted up his hands toward the people and blessed them, and he stepped down after making the sin offering and the burnt offering and the peace offerings. Moses and Aaron went into the tent of meeting. When they came out the Lord appeared to all the people. Then fire came out from before the Lord and consumed the burnt offering and the portions of fat on the altar; and when all the people saw it, they shouted and fell

on their faces.

The source of this consuming fire was easily understood and visually evident to Israel. When the fire "came out from before the Lord" it came from the very presence of God in their midst. The fire emerged from the pillar of fire and cloud which continually hovered over the tabernacle and indicated his divine presence. The fire that consumed the sacrificial offering was none other than God himself.

> Numbers 9:15 – 16 Now on the day that the tabernacle was erected the cloud covered the tabernacle, the tent of the testimony, and in the evening it was like the appearance of fire over the tabernacle, until morning. So it was continuously; the cloud would cover it by day, and the appearance of fire by night.

It was Jehovah who provided his special fire to be used on the altar of sacrifice and it was this fire, and only this fire, that was to be kept alive and used in the institutional offerings of the tabernacle. The priests were responsible for keeping it alive and for its sole use to the glory of God.

> Leviticus 6:12 – 13 The fire on the altar shall be kept burning on it. It shall not go out, but the priest shall burn wood on it every morning; and he shall lay out the burnt offering on it, and offer up in smoke the fat portions of the peace offerings on it. Fire shall be kept burning continually on the altar; It is not to go out.

We notice that twice in this passage is it mentioned, "It shall not go out." It was a solemn sacerdotal responsibility of the priests to keep the fire of God alive continually. Also the wonderful metaphor is seen here that each morning the priest was to place wood on the fire. It was and is today, the responsibility of God's priests and pastors to keep the fire of the altar of the spirit alive by continually stoking the flames each morning. For every pastor today, we should take great care to feed the flame of the Holy Spirit residing in us each and every morning through prayer and the study of the word of God.

THE FIRE OF PENTECOST

The same fire that consumed the sacrifices at the tabernacle in the wilderness, at the inauguration of the worship of the Lord in Sinai, was evident at the birthday and inauguration of the Christian Church on Pentecost of c. 30 AD, as the tongues of fire of the Holy Spirit appeared on every believer. God expects the same of us today as we are charged with the responsibility to keep those sacrificial altars in our hearts alive with the spiritual flames of the Holy Spirit granted to His people at Pentecost.

I Thessalonians 5:19 Do not quench the Spirit.

THE FIRE OF WORSHIP

Very early on in the sacrificial system of Israel, the Lord made it plainly evident to all that his authority and directives were to be taken seriously. In the object lesson learned regarding the casual service of Nadab and Abihu we learn that explicit obedience to God in all matters of his service is vitally important. We also see that God is not a respecter of persons in such matters, as these men were the sons of Aaron the high priest. After being instructed regarding the care and preservation of the fire provided by God for the service of the tabernacle, Nadab and Abihu casually and carelessly took other fire with them into the tabernacle for the daily ministration. We see the sad result of their indifference to divine command in Leviticus 10.

> Leviticus 10:1 – 3 Now Nadab and Abihu, the sons of Aaron, took their respective firepans, and after putting fire in them, placed incense on it and offered strange fire before the Lord, and fire came out from the presence of the Lord and consumed them, and they died before the Lord. Then Moses said to Aaron, 'It is what the Lord spoke saying, 'By those who come near Me, I will be treated as holy, and before all the people, I will be honored.'

It is important to note, that in the context of this treatise, the fire of God "consumed" Nadab and Abihu. The word of God says nothing of them being sent to the hell of excruciating eternal torment. Leviticus indicates that only their temporal lives were snuffed out by the powerful and all-consuming flame of God.

At Elijah's contest with the prophets of Baal at Mount Carmel, the same fire of God was evident at the consumption of Elijah's sacrificial offering. The presence of the Lord, by his fiery intervention, convinced Israel of his divine reality.

> I Kings 18:36 – 39 At the time of the offering of the evening sacrifice, Elijah the prophet came near and said, 'O Lord, the God of Abraham, Isaac and Israel, today let it be known that You are God in Israel and that I am Your servant and I have done all these things at Your word. Answer me, O Lord, answer me, that this people may know that You, O Lord, are God, and that You have turned their heart back again' Then the fire of the Lord fell and consumed the burnt offering and the wood and the stones and the dust, and licked up the water that was in the trench. When all the people saw it, they fell on their face; and they said, 'The Lord, He is God; the Lord, He is God.'

The matter of God's presence being demonstrated by consuming fire, at the inauguration of worship, is also seen at Solomon's dedication of the temple in Jerusalem. After Solomon's prayer of dedication the Lord made certain that no one was confused about the source of the divine acceptance of the temple and of Solomon's prayer.

> 2 Chronicles 7:1 – 3 Now when Solomon had finished praying, fire came down from heaven and consumed the burnt offering and the sacrifices, and the glory of the Lord filled the house. The priests could not enter into the house of the Lord because the glory of the Lord filled the Lord's house. All the sons of Israel, seeing the fire come down and the glory of the Lord upon the house, bowed down on the pavement with their faces to the ground, and they worshiped and gave praise to the Lord, saying, 'Truly He is good, truly His lovingkindness is everlasting.'

Besides indicating his approval of the establishment of the tabernacle, the temple, the rededication of Israel to honoring him and his disapproval of careless service, the Lord also demonstrated his greatness by the fiery consumption of his enemies. In 2 Kings 1:9 – 16 we see how the consuming fire of God was twice sent to consume fifty soldiers each time who were sent by King Ahaziah to arrest the prophet Elijah.

THE LAKE OF FIRE AS THE SECOND DEATH

At the judgment, those who adamantly refuse to serve the Lord will be annihilated by God's consuming fire. This biblical fact has been demonstrated with the Scriptures already cited thus far in chapter four and will be further demonstrated in those yet to be quoted. The Bible speaks far more about consumptive destruction of the wicked than about any hint of eternal suffering in hell. Symbolically, the greatest enemy of the Lord, Satan himself, along with the Beast and the False Prophet (likely demons who inhabited those human figures),[75] will be cast into the Lake of Fire. "This is the second death, the lake of fire" (Revelation 20:10 & 15).

We should carefully note that the wicked, who are cast into the lake of fire, suffer "the second death." "It is appointed for men to die once and after this comes judgment (Hebrews 9:27)." Since all mankind must suffer the first death, the second death, not eternal life in hell-fire, is final, as those adamantly opposed to serving the Lord are snuffed out of existence by being consumed in the fiery judgment of God. They will be put out of their own misery, and out of ours as well, since they will be obstinately opposed

---

[75] *Alan F. Johnson, Revelation, Volume 12 The Expositor's Bible Commentary. General Editor Frank E. Gaebelein. (Grand Rapids, Zondervan Publishing House, 1999), 576.*

to the ways of God. Why should they suffer under the rulership of Jesus for eternity if that would make them unhappy? That would be a fate worse than their temporary pain and suffering in the consumptive flames of the lake of fire.

The Wicked Become Ashes

The Old Testament testifies to the perspective of the wicked facing annihilation. The last book and chapter of our Christian Old Testament summarizes the teaching of the Scriptures on this subject:

> Malachi 4:1 – 3 'For behold, the day is coming, burning like a furnace; and all the arrogant and every evildoer will be chaff; and the day that is coming will set them ablaze,' says the Lord of hosts, 'so that it will leave them neither root nor branch. But for you who fear My name, the sun of righteousness will rise with healing in its wings; and you will go forth and skip about like calves from the stall. You will tread down the wicked, for they will be ashes under the soles of your feet on the day which I am preparing,' says the Lord of hosts.

Walter Wink sees the possibility of eternal death for the wicked. He believes that their final end can possibly be eternal non-existence.

> God's victory ushers in the judgment of the living and the dead. The righteous will inherit eternal life. The evil, eternal judgment, or alternatively, eternal non-being.[76]

The wicked being reduced to ashes seems to be rather final in terms of snuffing out the lives of those who ultimately reject God. There is no room here for those who are consumed in this flame as to their having an immortal soul. They are dead. They are separated from God forever because of their "eternal non-being." Since their suffering in the lake of fire does not continue forever and ever, ad nausium, then John can be inspired to write accurately of the time that follows this second death with these words which follow only three and four verses later:

> Revelation 21:3 – 4 And I heard a loud voice from the throne, saying, 'Behold, the tabernacle of God is among men, and He will dwell among them, and they shall be His people, and God Himself will be among them, and He will wipe away every tear from their eyes; and there will no longer be any mourning, or crying, or pain; the first things have passed away.'

How could this be a factual statement if there were still millions or

---

[76] *Walter Wink, The Human Being. (Minneapolis, Fortress Press, 2002), 159.*

billions of people who are forced to endure excruciating pain with obvious tears of mourning in a continual eternal suffering in the flames of hell forever and ever as is depicted by traditional Christian teaching? Obviously the two concepts are utterly incompatible. Scripture does not agree with traditional Christianity's adherence to platonic Greek philosophy. The lake of fire will consume the wicked and they will die. The lake of fire is the second death, not eternal life in the excruciating fires of hell. Their suffering will certainly be of a very limited duration and at the end of that fiery consumption their bodies will have been reduced to ashes.

Edward Fudge states well the case for ultimate destruction of the unrepentant wicked. When discussing the belief of traditionalism, which sees millions of sinners suffering in conscious torment for eternity, Fudge states the alternative biblical case for consumptive destruction.

> No, no – a thousand times no. God is indeed a 'consuming fire,' as both the Old and New Testaments tell us. He will punish those who refuse his salvation, and not one of them will escape. There will be degrees of punishment, and the destructive process will allow plenty of opportunity for that. But whatever conscious suffering may be involved, the unrighteous will all finally die. It will be just as God warned Adam in the Garden, as he told Ezekiel centuries later, as he said through Paul still later and as he twice said through John in the closing pages of Scripture: "the wages of sin is death." The soul that sins shall die. The final end of the lost is the lake of fire, which is the second death. Life or death – these are the final two alternatives. Both that life and that death will last forever.[77]

Only after that great conflagration has run its course and all the unrighteous are dead, can the prophetic truth of chapter 21:3 – 4 be fulfilled. Only when death no longer exists and no one anywhere is in a state of pain, can all tears be wiped away and mourning and crying no longer be found to exist. Revelation 21:3 – 4 denies the theory of everlasting suffering in hell fire.

Even the wonderful sweet Psalms of the Old Testament speak of the fiery consumption of the wicked. Psalm 97, for example, teaches us of the coming reign of the Lord on the earth. In verse three the psalmist was inspired to write of the coming fiery consumption of God's adversaries:

> Psalm 97:1 – 3 The Lord reigns, let the earth rejoice; let the many islands be glad, clouds and thick darkness surround Him;

---

[77] *Edward William Fudge and Robert A. Peterson. Two Views of Hell. (Downers Grove, Intervarsity Press, 2000), 81 – 82.*

righteousness and justice are the foundation of His throne. Fire
goes before Him and burns up His adversaries round about.

Psalm 104:35 illustrates the consumption of sinners from the earth. They will cease to exist. They will be no more.
> Let sinners be consumed from the earth and let the wicked be no more. Bless the Lord, O my soul. Praise the Lord!

The prophet Ezekiel speaks of the coming of the day when the King of Tyre will be turned to ashes. Not only will he be turned to ashes, he will cease to exist. There appears to be no room for the theory of the immortality of the soul in his case.
> Ezekiel 28:18 – 19 By the multitude of your iniquities, in the unrighteousness of your trade you profaned your sanctuaries. Therefore I have brought fire from the midst of you; it has consumed you, and I have turned you to ashes on the earth in the eyes of all who see you. All who know you among the peoples are appalled at you; you have become terrified and you will cease to be forever.

In David's final psalm, as recorded in II Samuel, he took comfort in the everlasting covenant established with him by the Lord. He also took comfort in the fact that the worthless would come to an ignominious end, being burned with fire.

II Samuel 23:7b "And they will be completely burned with fire in their place."

The entire Bible focuses on the destruction of the wicked rather than on their unending eternal and immortal life in suffering and pain in hell. Another such example is found in Psalm 73 where Asaph speaks of the "destruction" that awaits the unfaithful.
> Psalm 73:27 – 28 For, behold, those who are far from You will perish; You have destroyed all those who are unfaithful to You. But as for me, the nearness of God is my good; I have made the Lord God my refuge, that I may tell of all Your works.

The biblical position is one in which the wicked are not granted immortality. Neither does Scripture allow for them to have immortal souls from the beginning of their creation. Consequently, they are able to die and do in fact perish in the final destruction of those who, in the end, entirely refuse salvation in Jesus Christ.
> There is little in the NT to suggest a state of everlasting punishment, but much to indicate an ultimate destruction or dissolution of those who cannot enter into life: conditional immortality seems to be the

doctrine most consonant with the teaching of Scripture.[78]

To those who have been so steeped in the traditionalist view of the immortality of the soul and of everlasting conscious torment in hell for the wicked, it is obvious that the presentation of this work is both shocking and quite unbelievable. That result demonstrates to the conditionalist just how far the church has strayed from biblical truth. Clark Pinnock speaks elegantly regarding the Scriptural position on the nature of hell and its consumption of the unbelievers.

> The Bible does leave us a strong general impression in regard to the nature of hell – the impression of final, irreversible destruction, of closure with God. The language and imagery used by Scripture is so powerful in that direction that it is surprising that more theologians have not picked up on it before now. The Bible uses the language of death and destruction, of ruin and perishing, when it speaks of the fate of the impenitent wicked. It uses the imagery of fire that consumes whatever is thrown into it; linking together images of fire and destruction suggests annihilation. One receives the impression that "eternal punishment" refers to a divine judgment whose results cannot be reversed rather than to the experience of endless torment (i.e., eternal punishing). Although there are many good reasons for questioning the traditional view of the nature of hell, the most important reason is the fact that the Bible does not teach it. Contrary to the loud claims of the traditionalists, it is not a biblical doctrine.[79]

In the New Testament, in addition to Revelation 20, we see other prominent examples of fiery annihilation of the unbelievers. The chief apostle Peter speaks of the destruction of ungodly men on the day of judgment.

> 2 Peter 3:7 But by His word the present heavens and earth are being reserved for fire, kept for the day of judgment and destruction of ungodly men.

The writer of Hebrews also conveys the biblical fact of the ultimate consumption of God's adversaries. The fire of God will be the means of the execution of the death sentence upon the wicked.

> Hebrews 10:26 – 27 For if we go on sinning willfully after receiving the knowledge of the truth, there no longer remains a sacrifice for sins, but a terrifying expectation of judgment and the fury of a fire which will consume the adversaries.

---

[78] *E.G. Selwyn, The First Epistle of St. Peter.(London, Macmillan, 1961), 358.*
[79] *John F. Walvoord; Zachary J. Hayes; Clark H. Pinnock, Four Views On Hell. General Editor, William Crockett. (Grand Rapids, Zondervan, 1996), 144.*

Full Knowledge Of Salvation Will Be Given To All

We must also notice that in verse 26 we have been given a vital key to understanding God's justice. The fiery consumption of the wicked, in this case, comes only after they have received "the knowledge of the truth." Once we have received that instruction in full, but have deliberately rejected it, then there is no longer the possibility of Jesus' sacrifice being applied to the unbelievers who will then be annihilated in the all-consuming fires of God's judgment.

It is my contention, at this point, that partial knowledge is not what is being referred to in verse 26. The intention there appears to be that one must be granted full knowledge of the truth of God's offer of salvation before one is truly accountable for a decision for or against Christ. God will not sentence anyone to the lake of fire and permanent annihilation unless they reject him based on a full understanding of his offer of salvation. With that in mind, exposure to mere natural religion, exposure to the fact that there must be a God who exists, which is exhibited in nature and creation, is not enough to convict one who does not yet understand the concept of salvation in the Lord. Partial knowledge attained through many different venues, including attendance at church, is not enough to convict the ungodly. One must be fully taught the knowledge of the truth before being held accountable before the judgment seat of God.

The natural world does not convict one of his own fallen condition of sinfulness. The natural order does not convey the fact that we have a Savior who paid the penalty of sin with his own blood and redeemed us from death. Natural religion does not teach of the need to repent and accept Jesus Christ as one's Savior. Much more is needed in order to bring full knowledge of the truth to an ignorant soul.

The Bible states that the day is coming when all people will be fully taught the knowledge and truth of God. First of all we see this fact in the clearly eschatological eleventh chapter of Isaiah.

> Isaiah 11:9 They will not hurt or destroy in all My holy mountain, for the earth will be full of the knowledge of the Lord as the waters cover the sea.

This concept is repeated in Habakkuk the second chapter. This chapter too, is focused on the end of the age in its emphasis.

> Habakkuk 2:14 For the earth will be filled with the knowledge of the glory of the Lord, as the waters cover the sea.

In chapter fifty-four, the prophet Isaiah also looked forward in vision to the coming day when all would be taught of the Lord. This chapter's theme is centered on the kingdom of God and the blessings of the Lord that will accrue to Israel and to the whole world.

> Isaiah 54:13 All your sons will be taught of the Lord; and the well-being of your sons will be great.

ALL NATIONS WILL BE GRANTED FULL KNOWLEDGE OF SALVATION

Psalm 98 glorifies God for His wonders. One of those wonders is that the Lord will make known his righteousness and his salvation to all the nations.

> Psalm 98:1 – 3 & 8b – 9 O sing to the Lord a new song, for He has done wonderful things, His right hand and His holy arm have gained the victory for Him. The Lord has made known His salvation; He has revealed His righteousness in the sight of the nations. He has remembered His lovingkindness and His faithfulness to the house of Israel; all the ends of the earth have seen the salvation of our God….Let the mountains sing together for joy before the Lord, for He is coming to judge the earth; He will judge the world with righteousness and the peoples with equity.

We should note that, "He has revealed His righteousness in the sight of the nations." This is certainly an indication that they will all be taught of his salvation. In fact according to this psalm "all the ends of the earth have seen the salvation of our God." If He then is going to "judge the world in righteousness and the peoples with equity" he must actually live up to that word and be equitably righteous in his judgment. Clearly he will not judge critically those who have not been taught. These people will all be taught of the Lord, in full knowledge of his truth before they can be righteously and equitably called into account.

In Scripture we note that the world will be filled with the knowledge of the Lord as the waters cover the sea because the Lord will have appointed many servants to teach the gospel to a spiritually ignorant world. This will be the role of those who have come to Christ in full acceptance of salvation in him in this current age. Those who are genuinely converted Christians today will be the teachers, the kingly priests, who will teach all peoples in the kingdom age. The role of priests after all is to conduct worship and to teach the people the truth of God. The Apostle John sees that the people of God will be both "kings and priests" in the kingdom age.

> Revelation 1:6 And hath made us kings and priests unto God and his Father; to him be glory and dominion for ever and ever. Amen. (KJV)

> Revelation 5:10 And hast made us unto our God kings and priests; and we shall reign on the earth.(KJV)

> Revelation 20:6b but they shall be priests of God and of Christ, and shall reign with him a thousand years.(KJV)

This job description and spiritual opportunity alone ought to be a wonderful evangelical enticement for people to come to salvation in this age. How wonderful it will be to be in the employ of the Lord as a king and a priest to his people.

In the authoritative Scriptures of the Bible we have seen that both the Old and the New Testaments teach the destruction and the annihilation of the wicked. Scripture does not portray eternal suffering in hell as taught in traditional Christianity. Annihilation both portrays the seriousness of one's rejection of God in addition to demonstrating God's mercy, as he will extinguish the lives of the wicked in a relatively short period of time. God is not a sadist and will not subject the ignorant and the wicked to never-ending excruciating pain in hell for eternity. Rather he is just, righteous, merciful and equitable in his judgment of all of his children.

Michael Green questions traditional Christian teaching regarding the state of the lost. He neither accepts universalism nor the conscious unending torment and suffering of the lost in hell as genuinely Christian options.

> What sort of God would He be who could rejoice eternally in heaven with the saved while downstairs the cries of the lost make an agonizing cacophony? Such a God is not the person revealed in Scripture as utterly just and utterly loving. To be sure, the New Testament is emphatic about the possibility of eternal ruin. To be sure, it speaks about hell in a direct manner. But it does not teach the conscious unending torment of those who are eternally separated from God. The language of 'destruction' is the most common description of final loss in the Bible.[80]

In summary, in chapter four we see that God himself is the consuming fire that will ultimately annihilate the incurably wicked. The lake of fire, which is God himself, will bring about the second and final death in complete annihilation of those who refuse his offer of salvation. Through that process, which will last for a relatively short period of time, the wicked will be turned to ashes, and will thus suffer eternal punishment, rather than eternal punishing. Their punishment will include the fact that they will no longer be alive for eternity. They are dead because they have suffered the second death.

Consideration of the state of the dead is of foremost interest regarding

---

[80] Michael Green, *Evangelism Through The Local Church.* (Nashville, Thomas Nelson Publishers, 1992), 72.

Conditional Immortality. The next chapter will explore the perspectives on the intermediate state from an Old Testament Hebraic standpoint. This chapter will shed much light on whether Hebrew theology saw the state of the soul as being mortal or immortal, alive or asleep after physical death.

CHAPTER FIVE
THE OLD TESTAMENT VIEW OF DEATH

Chapter Five

The Old Testament View Of Death

*I go to slepe before you,
And wee shal wake together.*[81]

As mentioned at the end of chapter four we will now consider the state of the dead. This chapter will focus on the intermediate state of death from the standpoint of belief expressed in the Hebraic Scriptures of the Old Testament.

Sheol

In one of my seminary class sessions, the professor was discussing Genesis 42:38 which speaks of *sheol* and sorrow. He stated that this is one of the biblical texts which demonstrate that *sheol* is a place of sorrow.

According to *The Enhanced Strong's Lexicon*, the Hebrew *sheol* (St. # 7585), means grave or pit.[82] Both the King James Version and the New International Version translate *sheol* as "grave" for this verse. The New American Standard Bible transliterates *sheol*. It seems the sense of the usage of *sheol* here is simply a reference to the grave, not to a place of a shadowy and sorrowful existence.

In response to the professor's proclamation that the verse declared that *sheol* is a place of sorrow, this student offered that the passage is referring to the process of going to the grave as being a sorrowful experience rather than *sheol* itself being a place of sorrow. With a dumbfounded look he said, "Well, you'd better be prepared to defend that position then." So it is, that in this chapter, defense of my position regarding the state of the dead in *sheol* is set forth.

Conditional Immortality is dependent upon the dead being in a state of nonexistence, in a metaphorical sleep during the intermediate state. That is why we now will consider the biblical evidence on the state of the dead.

John Wenham speaks of Conditional Immortality and the idea that the lost will eventually cease to exist in what the Bible calls the second death. He also sees that paradise is heaven, the reward of the saved.

The other alternative, the possibility that the lost will eventually

---

[81] Bryan W. Ball, *The Soul Sleepers, Christian Mortalism from Wycliffe to Priestly.* (Cambridge, James Clarke & Co., 2008), 43. (Inscription on the tomb of Richard Rainoldes, words to his wife on the day of his death, 1582.)
[82] James Strong, *Enhanced Strong's Lexicon.* (Woodside Bible Fellowship, 1995), from Libronix Digital Library System, copyright 2004.

pass out of existence, needs much more serious attention. Conditionalists (as those who uphold conditional immortality are called) look for the resurrection of all men, followed by a just sentence according to the deserts of each, which will mean anguish (but not unending torment) for those outside Christ, finally terminating in the second death. Some (though not all) believe that there is no conscious existence of a soul-without-body between death and resurrection, but that at death all pass into a soul-sleep in total unconsciousness. This would mean that the first consciousness of the redeemed after death would be of Christ's welcome into paradise, that is to say, into heaven.[83]

While one may disagree with his assessment that the reward of the believers is a paradisical existence in heaven, my own position does agree that at death all enter into a soul-sleep of complete unconsciousness as explained previously. That soul-sleep is metaphorical since the soul, our mortal life, does not exist in the intermediate state.

Kenneth A. Matthews describes the "sorrow" of Jacob not as the condition of the place of *sheol*. Rather, "sorrow" is "the natural torment that he as a bereaved father would experience."[84]

Genesis 37:35 is another passage in which Jacob expresses the same idea. At the evidence of Joseph's coat covered with blood, Jacob assumed that Joseph was dead. He declared his sadness by saying: "Surely I will go down to *sheol* in mourning for my son." In this statement by Jacob, it is quite evident that he is referring to the process of going to the grave as being a sorrowful event. There is no indication in either of these Genesis accounts that *sheol* itself is a place of sorrow, only that the process of going to *sheol*, to death and the grave, is sorrowful. The process of death and dying is a sorrowful experience for any of us, and apparently this is what Jacob is considering.

Isaiah 26:19 gives insight into the biblical view of ancient Israel's perspectives on the realm of the dead. What is depicted as being in the earth is the body itself, the corpse, not the soul or spirit.

> Your dead will live; their corpses will rise, you who lie in the dust,
> awake and shout for joy, for your dew is as the dew of the dawn,
> and the earth will give birth to the departed spirits.

This is one of the most definitive verses in the Hebrew Scriptures regarding the coming resurrection of the dead. It is full of promise and

---

[83] John W. Wenham, *The Goodness Of God.* (London, Inter-Varsity Press, 1974), 34 – 35.
[84] Kenneth A. Matthews, *Genesis 11:27 – 50:26.* General Editor: E. Ray Clendenen. (Nashville, Broadman & Holman Publishers, 2006), 784.

encouragement that the "dead will live." Their hope is not lost. The day of their resurrection is promised for "their corpses will rise." Then we are given, once again, the biblical perspective that the dead are not cognizant but rather they are "asleep" since at the resurrection they shall "awake and shout for joy." Mention of "the dew of the dawn" speaks of the refreshing of life that will occur on that day just as a heavy dew nourishes the earth giving it newness of life. Rain and dew and the associated renewal of life were vital elements for the reinvigoration of both man and crops in Israel.[85]

Spirit, Body And Soul

The final phrase of this passage speaks of the earth giving "birth to the departed spirits." Lest one jump on this phrase and use it as a proof-text for the theological view that the spirits or souls of the dead reside in *sheol*, under the earth, we need to consider a number of issues. First, the passage does not speak of the spirits residing in the earth. Solomon, in the book of Ecclesiastes, tells us that the spirit in man returns to God who gave it. In Ecclesiastes three and verses 19 – 21 one can see that Solomon, first of all, hints at that idea that the spirit in man ascends to God in heaven.

> For the fate of the sons of men and the fate of beasts is the same. As one dies so dies the other; indeed, they all have the same breath and there is no advantage for man over beast, for all is vanity. All go to the same place. All came from the dust and all return to the dust. Who knows that the breath of man ascends upward and the breath of the beast descends downward to the earth?

Later, in chapter twelve, verses 5b – 7 we see Solomon's elaboration on the idea that the spirit of man returns to God upon death. His description of death is actually the reversal, the dissolution of the process of creation seen in Genesis 2:7.

> For man goes to his eternal home while mourners go about in the street. Remember Him before the silver cord is broken and the golden bowl is crushed, the pitcher by the well is shattered and the wheel at the cistern is crushed; then the dust will return to the earth as it was, and the spirit will return to God who gave it.

Paul House elaborates on this verse. He explains that in spite of the spirit's return to God that the human spirit is not Divine in the same sense as the Holy Spirit.

All life comes from God, so all life must return to God. This

---

[85] *John N. Oswalt, The Book of Isaiah, Chapters 1 – 39. Edited by R. K. Harrison. (Grand Rapids, William B. Eerdmans Publishing Co., 1986), 487.*

realization is not offered as a comforting comment here, but it does answer the question raised in 3:21 about the direction of the human spirit upon death as opposed to its animal counterpart. Stressing the human spirit's upward direction does place it in contrast to both the animal's breath and the dustbound, now useless, human body. Human spirit is not divine, though, despite its return to God. Rather it remains under the power of the One who created it.[86]

Lest we again jump to conclusions regarding verse 5b where Solomon speaks of a man going to "his eternal home while mourners go about in the street" one needs to consider the fact that in ancient Israel, the grave was looked upon in this sense as "the eternal home."

> The meaning of v 5b is fairly obvious. It registers the death of a human being who is deposited in the tomb ("everlasting home"), to the keening of the mourners.[87]

In verse 7 we see that the corpse, the "dust," returns to the earth but that the spirit, *ruwach*, the spirit of a rational being, returns "to God who gave it." This is the exact opposite of the creative act of God in forming Adam in Genesis 2:7. The Lord now recovers unto himself the gift that gave man life in the first place, the very breath of God.

> The process described here is the reversal of Gen 2:7. The end of life is the dissolution (not annihilation; the Israelites never speculated how the "I" was in Sheol; cf. Eccl 9:10). Humans return to the dust (Gen 3:19) whence they came, while the life-breath given by God returns to its original possessor. This is a picture of the dissolution, not of immortality, as if there were a *reditus animae ad Deum*, "the return of the soul to God." There is no question of the "soul" here, but of the life-breath, a totally different category of thought.[88]

Murphy mentions that we should compare his thoughts to Ecclesiastes 9:10 which speaks of the Scriptural fact that (including verse 5) the dead know nothing, do not have activity, planning, knowledge or wisdom. The entirety of mental capacity is absent from the dead.

> (vs. 5) For the living know they will die; but the dead do not know anything, nor have they any longer a reward, for their memory is forgotten. (vs. 10) Whatever your hand finds to do, do it with all your might; for there is no activity or planning or knowledge or wisdom in Sheol where you are going.

---

[86] Paul R. House, *Old Testament Theology*. (Downers Grove, IVP Academic, 1998), 479.
[87] Roland Murphy, *Ecclesiastes*. (Dallas, Word Books, Publisher, 1992), 119.
[88] Ibid, 120.

To the ancient Israelite mind, the soul was in existence only during this temporal life. Yehezkel Kaufmann, speaking of the changes to the Israelite perspectives that came about during the inter-testamental period, shows that there was a growing understanding and clarity as to the comprehension of the relationship of man to God.

> Against this background a radical change in the concept of the relationship of the soul to God takes place. The Biblical view is that such a relationship exists only during man's life on earth. Death, the realm of "impurity," severs man forever from contact with the holy, and hence from God. "The dead do not praise Yah nor all those who go down into Silence" (Psalms 115:7) – this is the prevailing conception in Biblical literature.[89]

Regarding Isaiah 26:19, the second great consideration needs to be the meaning of the wording "departed spirits." Harris, Archer and Waltke give in-depth coverage to the meaning of this Hebrew word, *repaim*.

> *Ghosts of the dead, shades*. A word and idea of Ugaritic origin, *rp'I*, which means "the dead inhabitants of the netherworld" is cognate to both Hebrew and Phoenician *repaim*. In grave inscriptions from Sidon, the kings Tabnith and Eshmunazar refer to the *repaim*, but this usage dates from Hellenistic times. The primary fact concerning the eight occurrences of the root in the OT is that it appears exclusively in poetic passages. Its use is prescribed as a "B" word or second synonym in parallel series. The most common parallelism is death (dead), ghosts (Prov 2:18; Isa 26:14, 19 a more complex poetic structure; Ps 88:10, 11 {H 11, 12}).
> …However, the ghost-like character of the dead is not so clear. Really, as the term refers to dead persons, the translation "dead ones" would fit very well in all cases. This does not deny that other passages refer to continuing life of the soul, but not necessarily in shadowy semi-existence.[90]

Notice that Harris, Archer and Waltke emphasize the fact that the "ghost-like character of the dead is not so clear." Rather they choose to use "dead ones" as a better translation of Isaiah 26:19. Consequently, understanding the correct usage of repaim in this verse helps to clarify the issue of whether the term refers to the spirit or the soul in sheol. In fact, Isaiah does not strengthen the idea of the immortality of the spirit-soul in this passage.

---

[89] *Yehezkel Kaufmann, Great Ages and Ideas of the Jewish People. Edited by Leo W. Schwarz (New York, The Modern Library, 1956), 87.*
[90] *Richard Laird Harris, Gleason L. Archer, Jr. and Bruce K. Waltke, Theological Wordbook of the Old Testament. (Chicago, Moody Press, 1980), 858.*

It is safe to say that Isaiah 26:19 definitely speaks of the dead being asleep until the day of resurrection when their corpses will rise in a state of joy. Their spirits are currently in the possession of God who gave them in the first place. He is the One who will reunite the body and the spirit together forming the renewed souls of the believers on the day of resurrection at the eschaton yet to come.

It is in the resurrection that we have our hope. Our hope is not to be found in a misguided belief of our immortal souls being transported to heaven upon death. The Scriptures do not indicate that we will bypass the resurrection and go directly to heaven, "do not pass go, do not collect $200." (A Monopoly game term of course!) Rather, we will wait in a metaphorical sleep in the grave until the glorious revelation of the King of kings and Lord of lords on the day of our revivification at the promised resurrection of the saints at Jesus' second coming.

> For now, it needs to be pointed out that the general orientation of the New Testament is one which is in continuity with the Old with regard to these facts: that the body and soul alike are subject to death; that there is no dualism between the immortal soul and the temporal body; and that the individual's hope for redemption from death lies in God alone, who is the Lord of both life and death rather than in personal immortality as an essential aspect of human existence. The gift of immortality is the gift of eternal life with God experienced as a unity of body and soul through resurrection from the dead.[91]

The spirit, the body and the soul are terms that should be far less confusing than they are to Christians. The major reason why most do not understand these issues very well is because of the variety of doctrinal positions and differing views among preachers and theologians alike. Hopefully this volume will bring some increased level of understanding on the matter to both myself and to my readers.

ENOCH

Regarding the Old Testament view of death, we must now seek to correct some errors in doctrine, which have made their way into Christianity. The first that needs to be addressed is the matter of Enoch and the fact that God "took him." Common theological perspectives proclaim that God took Enoch to heaven and that he did not face death.

Victor P. Hamilton expresses mainstream theology when he states that Enoch was "lifted aloft into God's immediate presence." He also states

---

[91] Ray S. Anderson, *Theology, Death And Dying.* (New York, Basil Blackwell Inc., 1986), 45.

"Enoch is the only person of whom it is not said that he died. Instead God took him."[92]

Gordon J. Wenham verifies his belief that, regarding the pre-flood world, that all died with the exception of Enoch.[93] Enoch was the only one to survive by being taken by God.

Keil and Delitzsch state that Enoch was carried away by God and was taken away to the paradise of heaven. With such a translation they state that Enoch did not therefore see death.[94]

These examples of the teaching in traditional Christianity regarding the translation of Enoch into heaven do not stand up to further Scriptural scrutiny. A passage that Keil and Delitzsch use to verify their belief is Hebrews 11:5.

> By faith Enoch was taken up so that he would not see death; and he was not found because God took him up; for he obtained the witness that before his being taken up he was pleasing to God.

Any exegete is hereby invited to simply read a few more verses in Hebrews 11 at verse 13. The entire list of Old Testament heroes of faith that are in this faith chapter, including Enoch, are referred to in this verse.

> All these died in faith, without receiving the promises, but having seen them and having welcomed them from a distance, and having confessed that they were strangers and exiles on the earth.

We notice in the very first phrase, "All these died in faith." Enoch is included in "all these." According to this Scripture, Enoch died. What possibly could the reference to Enoch not seeing death then refer? We can only conjecture, but we must remember that Enoch lived just a generation before the Noatian deluge. The reason that the Lord decided to send a flood was primarily because of the exceedingly great amount of lawlessness to be found in mankind.

> Genesis 6:5 – 7 Then the Lord saw that the wickedness of man was great on the earth, and that every intent of the thoughts of his heart was only evil continually. The Lord was sorry that He had made man on the earth, and He was grieved in His heart. The Lord said, "I will blot out man whom I have created from the face of the land, from man to animals to creeping things and to birds of the sky; for I am sorry that I have made them."

---

[92] Victor P. Hamilton, *The Book of Genesis Chapters 1 – 17*. (Grand Rapids, William B. Eerdmans Publishing Company, 1990), 257.
[93] Gordon J. Wenham, *Genesis 1 – 15*. (Waco, Word Books, Publisher, 1987), 146.
[94] C.F. Keil and F. Delitzsch, *Keil & Delitzsch Commentary on the Old Testament, Volume One*. (Peabody, Hendrickson Publishers, 1989), 125.

Enoch, a righteous man, was so intimate in his relationship with God that it is said of him that he "walked with God (Gen 5:24)." A man of his integrity would certainly become the target of evil men who probably conspired to put him to death. If this scenario were correct then one could easily see why God would take him out of that environment where he was in imminent danger of death. That is most likely the kind of death that both Genesis and Hebrews refer to.

PHILO

This is not a far-fetched scenario and conclusion when we understand what both Philo and Josephus say about the matter. First Philo speaks of God changing Enoch's place. He refers to him as "Enos, which means 'a man'"

> For Moses says, with reference to one who fled from the audacious innovations of the body, and who came over to the interest of the soul, "He was not found because God changed his place;" and by this enigmatical expression the two things are clearly intimated, the migration by the change of place, and the solitude by his not being found.[95]

By Philo's account God did not take Enoch to His heaven. Rather the Lord simply changed Enoch's place. Apparently the Lord simply moved Enoch to a safe place on earth where he would not face the threat of martyrdom. According to Hebrews 11:13, Enoch did later die a natural death at some safer location on the earth.

Scripture reveals that the fate of all men, including Enoch, is death. We see this biblical truth expressed in I Corinthians 15:22:

For in Adam all die, so also in Christ all will be made alive.

As descendents of Adam, as Enoch was, we are all subject to death. All human beings ever born of the line of Adam die. The only exception being believers who are alive at the second coming. Only that generation of believers will not see death but rather will be transformed from mortal to immortal at the return of Christ.

JOSEPHUS

The great first century Jewish historian Josephus also wrote of the disappearance of Enoch. In fact he speaks of both Enoch and Elijah regarding their disappearances.

---

[95] C. D. Yonge, translator, *The Works of Philo*. (Peabody, Hendrickson Publishers, 1993), 665.

> Now at this time it was that Elijah disappeared from among men, and no one knows of his death to this very day; but he left behind him his disciple Elisha, as we have formerly declared. And indeed, as to Elijah, and as to Enoch, who was before the Deluge, it is written in the sacred books that they disappeared; but so that nobody knew that they died.[96]

Traditional Christian theology may continue to promote the idea of Enoch going to heaven when God "took him", but that conclusion does not bear up under the scrutiny of Scripture nor under the attestation of the bright penetrating lights of non-biblical historical evidence. The greatest testimony of all comes from our Lord Jesus Christ, in conversation with Nicodemus. In his deeply spiritual discussion, Jesus said words that we do not seem to desire to hear today. In a clear statement about the state of the dead Jesus said:

> John 3:12 – 13 If I told you earthly things and you do not believe, how will you believe if I tell you heavenly things? No one has ascended into heaven, but He who descended from heaven; the Son of Man.

Jesus is the Son of Man. By His own word, only He has ascended to heaven. Why don't we just believe our Lord? He has far more credibility than Plato or Socrates, than Augustine or Calvin or any of us who follow traditional convention on this issue.

ELIJAH

The case of what happened to Elijah is likewise an enigma in Christianity. The common teaching and belief in traditional Christianity is that Elijah was carried alive into God's heavenly dwelling, and like Enoch, he did not see death. Keil & Delitzsch state it as well as anyone in this way:

> As God had formerly taken Enoch away, so that he did not taste of death, so did He also suddenly take Elijah away from Elisha, and carry him to heaven without dying.[97]

Since we have already taken into question the ascent of Enoch to God's heaven, and demonstrated with both Scripture and historic evidence that such a conclusion is without merit, therefore one must also question this incident with Elijah. Let's begin by investigating the matter of the word "heaven."

---

[96] *William Whiston, A.M., translator. Josephus Complete Works. (Grand Rapids, Kregel Publications, 1969), 197.*
[97] *C.F. Keil and F. Delitzsch, Keil and Delitzsch Commentary on the Old Testament, Volume III. (Peabody, Hendrickson Publishers, 1989), 294.*

The Hebrew word used here is *samayim* (Strong's #8064). Strong's Concordance defines the term in the following manner:

> To be lofty, the sky (as aloft; the dual perhaps alluding to the visible arch in which the clouds move, as well as to the higher ether where celestial bodies revolve); - air, astrologer, heaven, heavens.[98]

Jon D. Levenson uses this word, samayim, to explain that Elijah was not taken to the spiritual heavenly glory of God. Rather he sees that Elijah was taken up into the sky, which is only the atmosphere, which surrounds this earth.

> Where was Elijah after he "went up to heaven in a whirlwind" (2 Kgs. 2:11)? The Hebrew word samayim is better rendered "sky" than "heaven," since the latter term suggests a paradisiac abode unknown in the Hebrew Bible. One should therefore guard against the impression that our passage describes an ancient Israelite counterpart to the Christian belief in the Assumption, or Dormition, of the Virgin Mary, for example. For there is no reason to think that Elijah is here assumed into heavenly glory, rewarded for his service, or brought into the company of other righteous servants of God. Rather, the God of Israel, whose throne is in the sky, whisks his servant Elijah away from the earth and toward his own mysterious and unapproachable abode.[99]

Levenson also cautions that we should not take this passage as a proof-text regarding immortality. He demonstrates that Biblical evidence does not betray just where or in what condition Elijah is today.

> But where the Tishbite resides in the interim (if, that is, he did not die) is something the biblical sources never address. The story of Elijah's translation into the sky testifies to the power of God over death but says nothing about the nature of immortality.[100]

THREE HEAVENS

Levenson's focus on the sky, rather than the assumed spiritual heaven of God, gives us opportunity to consider some other options as well. We must evaluate the fact that in the Bible there are revelations of three heavens. They would be the atmosphere as the first heaven. Secondly, outer space, the

---

[98] *James Strong, Strong's Exhaustive Concordance of the Bible, Updated Edition. (Peabody, Hendrickson Publishers, Inc., 2007), 1584.*
[99] *Jon D. Levenson, Resurrection And The Restoration Of Israel. (New Haven, Yale University Press, 2006), 100 – 101.*
[100] *Ibid, 101.*

realm of the astronomical bodies, and thirdly the glorious heavenly abode of God. The Apostle Paul presents three heavens in 2 Corinthians 12:2

> I know a man in Christ who fourteen years ago – whether in the body I do not know, or out of the body I do not know, God knows – such a man was caught up to the third heaven.

Most likely the "man" that Paul saw was either an angel or a Christophany during the time that he was being taught by the Lord in Arabia. In I Corinthians 15:8 he speaks of the fact that the Lord had appeared to him as well, and probably in a venue in addition to the road to Damascus experience. The main point here is that he saw this "man" ascend to the third heaven. His obvious intent is to convey the idea that the third heaven is God's glorious heavenly paradise. Merrill F. Unger speaks more about this issue in his Bible Dictionary. Likewise he sees three Scriptural heavens.

> Scriptures evidently specify three heavens, since "the third heaven" is revealed to exist (II Cor. 12:2). It is logical that a third heaven cannot exist without a first and second. Scripture does not describe specifically the first and second heaven. The first, however, apparently refers to the atmospheric heavens of the fowl (Isa. 2:18) and clouds (Dan. 7:13). The second heaven may be the stellar spaces (Cf. Gen. 1:14 – 18). It is the abode of all supernatural angelic beings. The third heaven is the abode of the Triune God. Its location is unrevealed.[101]

When we read in 2 Kings 2:11 "And Elijah went up by a whirlwind to heaven," we are not necessarily reading of Elijah's ascension to God's glorious paradisical abode in the third heaven. The likelihood would be that Elijah was simply carried to another place on the face of this earth as Enoch in Genesis, had been carried in order to live out his life in relative peace and then finally face the natural occurrence of death to which all of us finally succumb. There is biblical evidence to this effect.

HEAVEN'S POSTAL SERVICE

J. Barton Payne mentions that the last recorded act of Elijah most likely took place in 852 BC. However, King Jehoram committed his crimes of fratricide four years later and it is at that time that Elijah sent Jehoram a letter condemning his actions and pronouncing judgment upon him.

> 2 Chronicles 21:12 – 15 Then a letter came to him from Elijah the prophet saying, "Thus says the Lord God of your father David,

---

[101] *Merrill F. Unger, Unger's Bible Dictionary. (Chicago, Moody Press, 1979), 463.*

> 'Because you have not walked in the ways of Jehoshaphat your father and the ways of Asa king of Judah, but have walked in the way of the kings of Israel, and have caused Judah and the inhabitants of Jerusalem to play the harlot as the house of Ahab played the harlot, and you have also killed your brothers, your own family, who were better than you, behold, the Lord is going to strike your people, your sons, your wives and all your possessions with a great calamity; and you will suffer severe sickness, a disease of your bowels, until your bowels come out because of the sickness, day by day,'"

We must note that this letter from Elijah speaks of Jehoram in the past tense regarding his not walking in the ways of David or in the ways of his righteous father Jehoshaphat. The murder of his family members is also spoken of in the past tense. In addition, the prophecy of his coming calamity and sickness is spoken of in future tense. Consequently it is apparent that Elijah composed this letter in the midst of Jehoram's eight-year reign, after his translation, which occurred before Jehoram's fratricidal crime. Jehoram had a reign of eight years (2 Chronicles 21:18 – 20) and died in 843 BC.

This letter comes to Jehoram at least four years[102] after the apparent transmission of Elijah to heaven. Heaven must have a wonderful postal service. But one must wonder why no one else among us has ever received a letter postmarked "Heaven." But of course, neither did Jehoram because Elijah was still on earth. Earlier we noted that Josephus commented regarding the fact that both Enoch and Elijah had disappeared "so that nobody knew that they died." Josephus did not speak of either of them being transported to God's heaven but goes on to reveal the contents of the letter and to verify the biblical account of this document.

> As he was doing this, and had entirely cast his own country laws out of his mind, there was brought him an epistle from Elijah the prophet which declared, that God would execute judgments upon him, because he had not imitated his own fathers, but had followed the wicked courses of the kings of Israel; and had compelled the tribe of Judah and the citizens of Jerusalem to leave the holy worship of their own God, and to worship idols, as Ahab had compelled the Israelites to do, and because he had slain his brethren, and the men that were good and righteous. And the prophet gave him notice in this epistle what punishment he should undergo for these crimes, namely, the destruction of his people, with the corruption of the king's own wives and children;

---

[102] *J. Barton Payne, The Wycliffe Bible Commentary. Charles F. Pfeiffer, Editor. (Chicago, Moody Press, 1977), 407.*

and that he should himself die of a distemper in his bowels, with long torments, those his bowels falling out by the violence of the inward rottenness of the parts, insomuch that, though he see his own misery, he shall not be able at all to help himself, but shall die in that manner. This it was which Elijah denounced to him in that epistle.[103]

Scripture reveals that Elijah's letter was composed and sent at least four years after Elijah's supposed ascendancy to heaven. Josephus verifies the facts of the letter. In addition, the sons of the prophets understood that Elijah had been taken from place to place in a similar manner in the past. That is apparently why they were insistent on going out to search for him in 2 Kings 2:15 – 17. Their concern and understanding regarding Elijah's transference was not without good precedent for in I Kings 18:11 – 12, Obadiah is sent by Ahab to find Elijah and Obadiah fears for his life when he finds Elijah. His fear is based on his understanding that Elijah is likely to be carried away by the Lord to a different location. In his conversation with Elijah, he fears going back to Ahab with word of where Elijah is to be found since Elijah can so easily escape by being carried by the spirit to a different place.

> I Kings 18:11 – 12 And now you are saying, 'Go, say to your master, "Behold, Elijah is here."' It will come about when I leave you that the Spirit of the Lord will carry you where I do not know; so when I come and tell Ahab and he cannot find you, he will kill me, although I your servant have feared the Lord from my youth.

In Scripture it is obvious that the people of that day knew that Elijah was periodically transported by the Spirit from one locale to another. Obadiah understood that fact, so did the sons of the prophets, and Josephus believed he was simply taken somewhere else on earth, not to God's heaven.

PHILLIP

The Spirit is not limited to this particular incident, nor restricted only with Elijah when it comes to the business of the supernatural transport of his servants from one place to another. In the New Testament we see a similar incident regarding the spiritual transport of Philip.

In the eighth chapter of Acts we read of the incident where Philip was used to evangelize the Ethiopian Eunuch. Using the book of Isaiah, which the eunuch was reading, Philip taught enough of the gospel to him to the

---

[103] *William Whiston, A.M., translator. Josephus Complete Works. (Grand Rapids, Kregel Publications, 1969), 201 – 202.*

point that he wanted to be baptized. Upon completion of the baptism, we notice that God then had another job for Philip to do and he provided the necessary transportation.

> Acts 8:38 – 40 And he ordered the chariot to stop; and they both went down into the water, Philip as well as the eunuch, and he baptized him. When they came up out of the water, the Spirit of the Lord snatched Philip away; and the eunuch no longer saw him, but went on his way rejoicing. But Philip found himself at Azotus, and as he passed through he kept preaching the gospel to all the cities until he came to Caesarea.

Azotus was some thirty miles from Philip's meeting place with the eunuch. The city was located on the Mediterranean coast and is also known as Ashdod. It appears that in these several instances that God is not incapable of moving his people from one location on the earth to another while transporting them by the power of his divine Spirit. It is also abundantly evident that neither Enoch nor Elijah were taken to God's heaven. They were simply transported in the realm of the first heaven, the atmosphere around this earth, where whirlwinds actually do occur. Those proof-texts fall far short of genuine veracity in convincingly establishing a plausible argument for human beings being assumed to heaven at the time of their death. It appears that the traditional Christian position on this matter needs some serious reexamination.

JOB

The Book of Job shows us that in the earliest days of man there was concern about life after death. He asked an age-old question, that we all consider, and then he also went on to answer that question himself.

> Job 14:14 If a man dies, will he live again? All the days of my struggle I will wait until my change comes. You will call and I will answer you; you will long for the work of your hands.

This quotation from Job reveals a great deal regarding the theology of the Patriarchal age of some four thousand years ago. First we notice that Job understood that there would come a time when he would be changed. Second, he realized that some day God would call him and that he would be able to answer God's call. Third, Job knew that God loves his creation and has a longing desire for "the work of your hands," implying a desire to have fellowship with his created human beings.

These are all important and significant factors regarding the time of the resurrection of the saints as we understand it in twenty-first century Christianity. Job goes on to give additional information regarding his perspective on the coming resurrection in chapter nineteen and verses twenty-five to twenty-seven.

> As for me, I know that my Redeemer lives, and at the last He will take His stand on the earth. Even after my skin is destroyed, yet from my flesh I shall see God; whom I myself shall behold, and whom my eyes will see and not another. My heart faints within me!

According to Anderson, this passage clearly denotes Job's future resurrected life on earth rather than in some heavenly residence. Likewise it does not admit any sort of continued spiritual reality and presence after the death of the mortal body. Rather, Job understands that in that resurrection he will see God "from his flesh." Job understands the bodily resurrection.

> Even the startling passage in Job 19:25 does not directly speak of resurrection in the sense of life beyond death. 'For I know that my Redeemer lives, and at last he shall stand upon the earth; and after my skin has been destroyed, then from my flesh I shall see God, whom I shall see on my side.' At most, this passage affirms that God will be his advocate and the source of this life on earth. It does not look to continuation of life apart from some form of continued earthly existence.[104]

This passage more clearly defines Job's thoughts about the resurrection. First, he knows there is a Redeemer. Second he understands that that Redeemer will stand on the earth. Third, though he knows that there will be a passage of some indeterminate time, in which his flesh will decay, that yet his flesh will later be restored to him and that he will behold his Redeemer with his own restored eyes. No wonder Job was faint! From the perspective of four millennia ago we must admit that Job had a rather well defined theology of the return of the Lord, our Redeemer, who will claim and reconstitute his departed people at the resurrection of the second coming.

DANIEL AND THE JUDGMENT

In addition to Job, some of the strongest evidence of ancient knowledge of the state of the dead and of the resurrection is found in the book of the Prophet Daniel. We have biblical evidence that this prophecy was actually written by the Prophet Daniel and consequently that the dating of the book is from the 6th century BC, by the very words of Jesus in Matthew 24:15.

Therefore when you see the abomination of desolation which was

---

[104] *Ray S. Anderson, Theology, Death And Dying. (New York, Basil Blackwell Inc., 1986), 42.*

spoken of through Daniel the prophet, standing in the holy place (let the reader understand),

In that statement Jesus confirms two important points regarding the Book of Daniel. First, that Daniel is the author. Second, since Daniel is the author then it follows that it was written during Daniel's lifetime in the sixth century BC. These facts are often disputed by more liberal theologians and yet it becomes apparent that they do have an agenda in the denial of Daniel's authorship in that they want to assign it to an unknown writer in perhaps the second century BC. Dr. Thomas Rodgers pinpoints the apparent reasoning for their approach.

> Probably no other book in the Old Testament has been maligned by critics as much as the book of Daniel. But be encouraged, because it will stand on its own. It can be analyzed from linguistics; it can be analyzed from knowledge of the historical period in which Daniel lived; it can be analyzed from the prophecies contained therein. They all serve to validate that Daniel was a historical character and that he did write his book in the sixth century B.C. The reason why skeptics want to give the book a later date, is that they simply cannot believe that Daniel would be able to prophesy as accurately as he did about the nations which would succeed the Babylonian empire.[105]

In Daniel we witness the revelation of the resurrection as well as the judgment. In Daniel 7:9 – 10 we see the stage being set for the judgment time of mankind.

> I kept looking until thrones were set up, and the Ancient of Days took His seat; His vesture was like white snow and the hair of His head like pure wool. His throne was ablaze with flames, its wheels were a burning fire. A river of fire was flowing and coming out from before Him; thousands upon thousands were attending Him, and myriads upon myriads were standing before Him; the court sat, and the books were opened.

This passage corresponds almost exactly with the judgment scene in Revelation 19:11 – 19. In this case, the "Ancient of Days" is likely a reference to the Father. This judgment scene focuses specifically on the Beast, apparently a human being, who in verse eight has the eyes of a man and who utters great boasts. His lot is to be "slain and its body was destroyed and given to the burning fire." However, and this point is of immense importance in verse twelve, the other beasts are not similarly destroyed but

---

[105] *Thomas R. Rodgers, D.Min., The Panorama of the Old Testament. (Newburgh, Trinity Press, 2003), 337.*

rather it is stated that "an extension of life was granted to them for an appointed period of time." We must ask an important question. Why would these rulers of the final age of rebellious men, who oppose Christ at his return, be granted an extension of life?

If Paul's statement in Acts 17:30 is true, then we can perhaps begin to comprehend that these beasts are indeed ignorant of the true God, at least to the degree that is required for salvation, and they are being granted an extension of life in order to have a genuine opportunity to become believers and to accept Jesus as Lord and Savior. If God truly overlooks our ignorance, then he must be fair and apply it to these spiritually ignorant beast rulers as well. On the other hand, in such a scenario, the beast who was cast into the burning fire, must have been previously exposed to an adequate amount of saving knowledge, and with full saving knowledge having rejected it, in order to merit annihilation.

Verses twenty-four through twenty-seven appear to be a restatement of verses nine through eleven of the same chapter. Here we see that in the judgment the first beast's "dominion will be taken away, annihilated and destroyed forever." In verse eleven "the beast was slain, and its body was destroyed and given to the burning fire." From these two separate statements we understand four points regarding this beast:

1. His dominion is taken away
2. He is Slain
3. His body is destroyed and given to the burning fire
4. The word "annihilated" is used

ANNIHILATION

The Bible often speaks of the destruction of the wicked. Destruction is a synonym to the word annihilate. They both convey the same basic idea. If a person is destroyed or annihilated they are assumed to be dead. They have no further existence. This is the condition of those who are cast into the Lake of Fire. They are annihilated, they are destroyed and they cease to exist. These are not words that convey the idea of immortality in an ever-burning hell fire.

The Old Testament adequately and continually exhibits the idea of the destruction and finality of death, which will be the lot of the wicked. This position stands in marked contrast to mainline theology, which thus far in this book, has offered inadequate explanation in the light of Scripture. Clark H. Pinnock throws down the gauntlet to those who refuse to see the biblical perspective while continuing to favor the views of traditionalism.

> The Bible gives a strong impression to any honest reader that hell denotes final destruction, so the burden of proof rests with those who refuse to believe and accept this teaching.[106]

The preponderance of Scriptural evidence on this matter leads to one conclusion. Annihilation is the teaching of the Bible.

RESURRECTION IN THE OLD TESTAMENT

When Jesus and Martha discussed the matter of the resurrection of Lazarus, Martha made a forthright statement which demonstrated her theological view on the matter of the state of the dead and the coming renewal of life. Her answer was both emotional and abrupt indicating that it ejaculated forth from her deepest convictions.

> John 11:23 – 24 Jesus said to her, "Your brother will rise again."
> Martha said to Him, "I know that he will rise again in the resurrection on the last day."

How did Martha know that Lazarus would "rise again in the resurrection on the last day?" One of the major sources of her Scriptural understanding is found in the Book of Daniel. In Daniel the twelfth chapter the Scripture speaks plainly of this coming event.

> Daniel 12:1 – 3 Now at that time Michael, the great prince who stands guard over the sons of your people, will arise. And there will be a time of distress such as never occurred since there was a nation until that time; and at that time your people, everyone who is found written in the book, will be rescued, many of those who sleep in the dust of the ground will awake, these to everlasting life, but the others to disgrace and everlasting contempt. Those who have insight will shine brightly like the brightness of the expanse of heaven, and those who lead the many to righteousness, like the stars forever and ever.

We must notice that those who are dead are "asleep." This is the common expression of the state of the dead in the Old Testament and of the New Testament alike according to the teachings of Jesus, the Apostle Paul, and the early church. As a matter of fact Paul quotes a contemporary first century Christian hymn in Ephesians 5 which demonstrates the theology of death held by the first century Christian Church, the Church contemporaneous

---

[106] *Walvoord, John F., Hayes, Zachary J. and Pinnock, Clark H., Four Views On Hell. General Editor, Crockett, William. (Grand Rapids, Zondervan 1996), 145.*

with the Apostles of Christ including Paul himself.[107] Without question this hymn verse promotes the true gospel and the genuine theology of Jesus our Lord.

> Ephesians 5:14 For this reason it says, "Awake, sleeper, and arise from the dead, and Christ will shine on you."

Speaking of those in the state of death, Paul and the church refer to those who need to "awake" as being in a state of repose as a "sleeper." We must keep in mind that the context is the state of the dead at the time of the resurrection, "arise from the dead, and Christ will shine on you." Clearly, in the first century Church, the theology of believers focused on the dead being asleep, and the notion that they would awaken at their arising from the dead at the second coming. This was also the world and theology in which Martha was immersed. As a result of this background she was able to state to Jesus, without equivocation, that her brother Lazarus, "will rise again in the resurrection on the last day."

Ezekiel's Valley Of Dry Bones

One of the most powerful examples in the Old Testament pertaining to the resurrection of the dead and the eventual offer of salvation to all is found in Ezekiel thirty-seven. In this chapter we see the vision of the valley of dry bones. In this vision, Ezekiel is a participant and God used him to prophecy to the valley of dry bones. It seems that these bones represent Israel of great antiquity since in verse two we read that the bones were "very dry." As Ezekiel is called upon to systematically prophecy regarding their being granted flesh and skin and breath, these bones, which were dead, come back to life as the "whole house of Israel."

The resurrection of Ezekiel 37 of the "whole house of Israel" and of David in chapter 34:23-24 are certainly for the kingdom of God eschatonal age. Jan Levenson sees these resurrections as the time of restoration to physical life, not a reincarnation, as seen in pagan philosophy, but rather a restoration to life as the same persons they were in this age.

> This is obviously not reincarnation. For that term implies that the ancient Israelites believed in something like the later Jewish and Christian "soul" or like the notion (such as one finds in some religions) of a disembodied consciousness that can reappear in another person after its last incarnation has died. In the Hebrew

---

[107] *A. Skevington Wood, Ephesians, from The Expositor's Bible Commentary, Volume 11. Frank E. Gaebelein, General Editor. (Grand Rapids, Zondervan Publishing House, 1984), 70 – 71.*

Bible, however, there is nothing of the kind.[108]

In the text of Ezekiel thirty-seven these bones were so dried that they had no hope. The process of their restoration mirrors the creation of Adam in Genesis 2:7 as the corpses are rebuilt and finally the breath of God fills them and they come back to life.

In verses 12 – 14 it becomes obvious that this whole vision has to do with the resurrection from the dead of all Israel at the general resurrection of the eschaton. It could only represent the great general resurrection as the first resurrection is clearly only for those who were believers in this age. Certainly not all of Israel are believers in this age.

> Therefore prophecy and say to them,' Thus says the Lord God, "Behold, I will open your graves and cause you to come up out of your graves, My people; and I will bring you into the land of Israel. Then you will know that I am the Lord when I have opened your graves and caused you to come up out of your graves, My people. I will put My Spirit within you and you will come to life, and I will place you on your own land. Then you will know that I the Lord, have spoken and done it," declares the Lord!

This vision and prophecy corresponds well to the thinking of Paul in Romans. In Chapter 11:25 – 27 he deals with the matter of the salvation of Israel in comparison to the salvation of the Gentiles. He makes it plain that God has allowed a partial hardening of heart to come upon Israel but only until a certain time.

> For I do not want you, brethren, to be uninformed of this mystery – so that you will not be wise in your own estimation – that a partial hardening has happened to Israel until the fullness of the Gentiles has come in; and so all Israel will be saved; just as it is written, "the Deliverer will come from Zion, He will remove ungodliness from Jacob." This is My covenant with them, when I take away their sins."

Paul recounts the covenantal relationship that God established with Israel anciently. He also points out that "the gifts and the calling of God are irrevocable (vs. 29)." God's covenant with Israel and his calling them to be his special people has not been abrogated and God will be true to his word. Indeed, in spite of the fact that Israel was hard of heart at that time and during this age as well, the day will come when they will all return to the Lord and once again, in full acceptance of him, be his people.

---

[108] Jon D. Levenson, *Resurrection And The Restoration Of Israel*. *(New Haven, Yale University Press, 2006),110.*

Lloyd Gaston provides keys as to why all Israel will be saved. In short, they will be saved because God is faithful to his covenantal promises and that Israel is beloved for the sake of their forefathers. In addition the Lord will save Israel because it is out of Zion, out of Israel, that our Redeemer has come and he cherishes his own people.[109]

In Ezekiel 37 we witness the fact that "the whole house of Israel" will be resurrected and brought back to covenantal relationship with the Lord. Likewise, we notice in Romans 11 the very same phenomenon established in the New Testament that "all Israel will be saved."

Though Israel was not saved during Ezekiel's day and it was not saved in Paul's day, nor to any great degree is Israel saved in our day, it is thus required by Scripture that they will be saved in a yet future day. That day is then of necessity, most likely during the eschatonal kingdom of God. It is during that age, yet to come, in which God will stretch forth his gracious hand and grant time and opportunity for Israel to be taught the way of the Lord. Speaking of that time, the Holy Spirit inspired Jeremiah the prophet to foretell an age of renewal and a new covenantal relationship that would exist between the Lord and his people Israel.

> Jeremiah 31:31 – 34 'Behold, days are coming,' declares the Lord, 'when I will make a new covenant with the house of Israel and with the house of Judah, not like the covenant which I made with their fathers in the day I took them by the hand to bring them out of the land of Egypt, my covenant which they broke, although I was a husband to them,' declares the Lord. 'But this is the covenant which I will make with the house of Israel after those days,' declares the Lord, 'I will put My law within them and on their heart I will write it; and I will be their God, and they shall be My people. They will not teach again, each man his neighbor and each man his brother, saying, 'Know the Lord,' for they will all know Me, from the least of them to the greatest of them,' declares the Lord, 'for I will forgive their iniquity, and their sin I will remember no more.'

The writer of Hebrews repeats this prophecy in 8:8 – 12 almost verbatim. Consequently we can see that this doubled prophecy is both of Old and New Testament promise and perspective. In that day "they will all know Me," is the promise of the Lord for his people Israel. In the kingdom age to come, all Israel will know the Lord and "all Israel will be saved."

Is this principle and promise available only to Israel and not to the Gentiles?

---

[109] Lloyd Gaston, *The Romans Debate*, Editor, Karl P. Donfried. (Peabody, Hendrickson Publishers, 1991), 323.

It would be very hard indeed to visualize that God would make salvation available for one ethic group in the general resurrection of the kingdom age but not for the rest of mankind. Perhaps another principle that Paul supplies is at work in this case. Perhaps salvation will be offered to all those Israelites who had been blinded in this age to the truth of the gospel, and according to Acts 17:30, those Gentiles who were ignorant of the Lord will also be granted opportunity for salvation in the age to come. After all, Paul said twice in the book of Romans, "to the Jew first and also to the Greek (Romans 1:16 & 2:10)." In God's dealing with mankind he has always honored the precedent of offering salvation first to his chosen people Israel and then to the Gentiles. Should we expect it would be any different in the eschatological kingdom?

The main point here is the biblical fact that in the kingdom age all will have opportunity for salvation who did not have it in this current age. Ignorance will be replaced with full knowledge of the Lord and his plan of salvation. Mankind in general will finally be granted abundant opportunity to make a studied rational decision regarding their choosing or rejecting salvation offered in Jesus Christ.

Pharisaistic Concept Of Death

During the ministry of Jesus there appeared divergent views among the principle religious factions in Judea. The Sadducees formed the more conservative sect of Judaism and rejected the existence of angels and demons and also rejected the idea of resurrection and any life beyond death. On the other hand the Pharisees held to belief in a future state after death and they believed in a coming resurrection. Their thoughts concerning the resurrection were also highly influenced by Greek philosophy, which had become a major part of Israelite religious views during the intertestamental period largely because of the significant inroads made through the Hellenization of Palestine after Alexander.

> The OT has little specific to say about the future state of the individual after death. Greek thought sharply divided between the soul and the body, the soul's temporary prison, and saw immortality as a quality of the soul. The Pharisees leaned toward a belief in resurrection that owed more to Greek ideas than to the OT. However, the Sadducees refused to even face the clear implications of OT teaching about the future state and were skeptical of the nature of personal future existence related to rewards or punishment. [110]

[110] *Walter L. Liefeld, Luke, The Expositor's Bible Commentary, Volume 8. Frank E. Gaebelein, General Editor. (Grand Rapids, Zondervan Publishing House, 1984), 1016.*

It was during the Hellenistic period that the concept of the immortality of the soul began to be noticed in the religion of the Jewish people. One must keep in mind that this concept had no historic precedence in Israelite religion but rather it became an issue with the onslaught of Greek influence.

> In the third and second centuries B.C.E. we also hear for the first time of immortality and resurrection as the rewards that await the righteous, and of eternal punishments that await the wicked. In the pre-exilic portions of the Bible, *sheol* is the ultimate destination for the disembodied souls of everyone, righteous and wicked alike. In Sheol, much like the Greek Hades, there is no judgment and no reward. A few poetical passages imply that God can bring back from Sheol those who have been consigned there (I Sam. 2;6), or that the dead might live again (Isa. 26:19; Ezek. 37:1 – 14), but these are metaphorical expressions of God's prowess, not crucial elements in a system of theodicy.[111]

The heavy influence of Greek philosophy, so prevalent in the world, was a snare to some early second and third century Christians who sought to teach Christianity to the pagan world from the perspective of the Grecian Platonic mindset. In the long run this teaching became a negative influence and presented a perversion of basic Christian biblical truth. This perversion of the gospel is noticed regarding the nature of the soul and matters of a future life.

William Crockett cites an older printing of Fudge's *The Fire That Consumes*, in which Fudge argues that the Greek influence on the teaching of *hades* and the immortality of the soul, became part of church teaching and doctrine. He places the major influence of Platonism as developing in the first three centuries of the Christian Church.

> Many Christian writers of the second and third centuries...wrapped their understanding of Scripture in the robes of philosophy. Paul had often warned against contemporary philosophy (I Cor. 1:19 – 2:5; Col. 2:1 – 10), but these apologists, zealous for their new-found faith, set out to battle the pagan thinkers on their own turf.[112]

The perspective that the soul is immortal began to be an accepted part of Christian Theology early in church history. Such a position was never found in the Old Testament and its incorporation brought about a perverted view of New Testament Theology and the presentation of the gospel. Christian Theologians thereafter had to find convenient places to store the immortal

---

[111] *Shaye J.D. Cohen, From the Maccabees to the Mishnah. (Philadelphia, The Westminster Press, 1987), 91.*
[112] *William V. Crockett, General Editor, Four Views On Hell, Chapter Two, The Metaphorical View. (Grand Rapids, Zondervan, 1996), 67.*

souls of those who had died. One way to handle the problem, and this is evidently the case, was to speed up the biblical chronology and have the souls of the believers go to heaven at physical death and the souls of the unfortunate unbelievers go to hell. This sped-up process then bypassed the biblical resurrections and their consequences while maintaining the adoption and inclusion of the philosophy, of pagan origin, regarding the immortality of the soul.

In summary, we note that the primary usage of the Hebrew *sheol* is that of the burial place of the dead. It is not a place of shadowy existence in a state of sorrow. We have seen that the soul is the indwelling of the breath of God in combination with the body, which in union make the soul or life. The proof texts of Enoch and Elijah being taken to heaven are dealt with and seen to be wanting in any attempt to prove that believers go to heaven upon death. The "heaven" referred to is in the end most likely a reference to the atmosphere through which both Enoch and Elijah were moved as God simply took them to another place on earth. In the life of Philip, he too was likewise transported to another place where he was to continue his ministry. The prophet Job understood the resurrection and that he would be revitalized on that day. Likewise Daniel speaks of the resurrection followed by the day of judgment. Neither Job nor Daniel saw anything of the reward of heaven for believers. Martha, the sister of Lazarus, understood there would be a resurrection coming, according to her understanding of the Scriptures in her day. Ezekiel's vision of the valley of dry bones indicates to us that Israel is not in heaven, and that their only hope is in the coming resurrection, at which time they will be given new life and opportunity for salvation. The Pharisees too, though they opposed the ministry of Jesus, were much in line with Jesus' teachings of the coming resurrection.

The groundwork is now concluded in preparation for our focus on the New Testament view of death, and resurrection and how it influences the doctrinal arguments for Conditional Immortality. We will discover, in chapter six, how Jesus refers to the state of the dead and their opportunity for salvation. In addition we will read the perspectives of some of the major movers of the Protestant Reformation on the subject.

Chapter Six
The New Testament View Of Death

Chapter Six
The New Testament View Of Death

For this reason it says,
"Awake sleeper,
and arise from the dead,
and Christ will shine on you."
Ephesians 5:14

In the interest of establishing a biblical case for the doctrine of Conditional Immortality we must consider the New Testament teaching on the state of the dead. If indeed all who never came to accept salvation in Jesus Christ, who died outside the faith, are in fact at this moment suffering excruciatingly endless pain and agony in the fires of hell, then there is no valid case for my theological viewpoint. Conditional Immortality is dependent upon Scriptural proof of the mortality of the soul and of its metaphorical lifeless sleep during the intermediate state.

Since the majority of mankind has not been reached with genuine full instruction and opportunity for salvation, then by default they are lost according to the majority theological view. That is, if one subscribes to the dogma of traditional Christian Theology.

In this chapter we will explore a far more merciful course, outlined by our Savior himself, by the Apostle Paul and by the testimony and acknowledged support rendered by a number of Conditionalists who have bravely contributed to a more universal theology.

Jesus' Teaching On The State Of The Dead

Lazarus

Jesus' friend, Lazarus of Bethany, was sick and nearing death. His sisters, Mary and Martha, sent word to Jesus that their brother, whom Jesus loved, was sick. In response to this urgent appeal to Jesus to come to their brother, Jesus continued for two more days before traveling to Bethany. Such apparent disregard for Lazarus and his health was unbelievable to his sisters and they each accusatorily blamed Jesus for not coming earlier, with these words:

> John 11:21 & 32 Lord, if you had been here, my brother would not have died.

Was Jesus so callous and uncaring about this family, which he dearly loved? Did he delay coming to them because he had other pressing matters to deal with? No, on the contrary, Jesus saw the bigger picture and the opportunity to glorify God in the process of how he dealt with Lazarus and the family.

> Vs. 4 But when Jesus heard this, He said, 'This sickness is not to end in death, but for the glory of God, so that the Son of God may be glorified by it.'

> Vs. 40 Jesus said to her, 'Did I not say to you that if you believe, you will see the glory of God?'

The letter of Mary and Martha was written with urgent appeal since they knew that Jesus had the power to heal by the many examples in his ministry. After Jesus received this letter from the sisters he told his disciples:

> Vss. 11b – 14 'Our friend Lazarus has fallen asleep; but I go, so that I may awaken him out of sleep.' The disciples then said to Him, 'Lord, if he has fallen asleep, he will recover.' Now Jesus had spoken of his death, but they thought that He was speaking of literal sleep. So Jesus then said to them plainly, 'Lazarus is dead.'

The Lord clearly taught in this example that the state of death was like being asleep. He did so without reference to whether the soul was still in existence in an intermediate state. In addition we note that it is not recorded that Lazarus came back to resurrected life speaking of what it was like to be in heaven, hell, purgatory, *sheol* or any shadowy intermediate state. If he had been in heaven, consider how disappointed he would have been to once again be limited to his mortal earthly existence. The basic principle of Old Testament Theology on the matter of the state of dead mortal men is found in Psalm 146:3 – 4.

> Do not trust in princes, in mortal men, in whom there is no salvation. His spirit departs, he returns to the earth; in that very day his thoughts perish.

The wisest of all mortal men, King Solomon, wrote definitively regarding the state of the dead. In Ecclesiastes 9:5 and 10 he speaks of the mental capability of the deceased.

> Vs 5 For the living know they will die; but the dead do not know anything, nor have they any longer a reward, for their memory is forgotten.

> Vs 10 Whatever your hand finds to do, do it with all your might; for there is no activity or planning or knowledge or wisdom in *sheol* where you are going.

The author of Psalm 146 goes on to speak of the dead in *sheol* as being "in the land of forgetfulness." In consideration of that "land of forgetfulness" where ones' "thoughts perish" and where the dead do not know anything, one can begin to understand that with Scriptural authority Jesus considered that the dead are "asleep."

George R. Beasley-Murray, in commenting about John 11:11 – 12, sees Jesus' statement to his disciples regarding Lazarus being asleep to be indicative of the state of death from which we will be resurrected and revitalized at the second coming. According to him, the sleep of death was to the Hebrew mind a state from which there was no awakening.

> An ambiguous statement of truth is misunderstood by the hearers, which leads to a clarification that opens up fuller revelation. That Lazarus has "fallen asleep" employs a familiar image of death, but in the Hebrew heritage it chiefly connoted a sleep from which there is no awakening…With Jesus the thought is fundamental, bound up with the relation of God to his people and his own role as the Son who is Son of Man. Hence he declares, "Lazarus has fallen asleep; I am going to wake him out of sleep!" The same outlook on death is seen in Mark 5:39, as Jesus advances to wake a child from death, just as he was to wake Lazarus. The idea was as ridiculous to the mourners for the child as it was distant from those who mourned Lazarus. In this context the implication of v 11 should be taken with utmost seriousness, particularly in light of vv 25 – 26; believers are to view death as a sleep from which they shall be awakened through Jesus.[113]

---

[113] George R. Beasley-Murray, *John, from the Word Biblical Commentary.* (Nashville, Thomas Nelson Publishers, 1999), 188-189.

Oscar Cullmann, a famed Conditionalist of the mid-twentieth century, spoke of the theological options regarding the state of the dead. He noted the incompatibility of the acceptance of both the immortality of the soul and the biblical position of the resurrection of the dead after their sleep in the grave. He addressed this major point of contention in his writings.

> For many of those who have attacked me the cause of 'sorrow and distress' has been not only the distinction we draw between resurrection of the dead and immortality of the soul, but above all the place which I with the whole of primitive Christianity believe should be given to the intermediate state of those who are dead and die in Christ before the final days, the state which the first-century authors described by the word 'sleep'.[114]

Cullman noted that later Christianity found a link between the two concepts. However, that reasoning was unconvincing to him. His repudiation of this view saw in it the furtherance of the immortality of the soul as being opposed to the resurrection teaching of the Bible and that it was simply a continuation of pagan Greek philosophy and its heavily negative influence on the theology of the Christian Church.

> The fact that later Christianity effected a link between the two beliefs and that today the ordinary Christian simply confuses them has not persuaded me to be silent about what I, in common with most exegetes, regard as true; and all the more so, since the link established between the expectation of the 'resurrection of the dead' and the belief in the 'immortality of the soul' is not in fact a link at all but renunciation of one in favour of the other. I Corinthians 15 has been sacrificed for the Phaedo.[115]

The Apostle Paul, in writing his epistle to the Ephesian Church, quotes from a first century Christian hymn that was possibly associated with the baptism of new converts. The contents of Ephesians 5:14 may have been borrowed from Isaiah 26:19, "your dead will live, their corpses will rise," and perhaps also from Isaiah 60:1 "Arise, shine; for your light has come, and the glory of the Lord has risen upon you."

> Ephesians 5:14 For this reason it says, "Awake, sleeper, and arise from the dead, and Christ will shine on you."

N.T. Wright agrees that Ephesians 5:14 is an early Christian poem or hymn. He sees that it has to do with both Jesus' heavenly and earthly life, which can also be ours.

---

[114] *Oscar Cullmann, Immortality of the Soul or Resurrection of the Dead? (London, Epworth Press, 1964), 10.*
[115] *Ibid, 7 – 8.*

> Ephesians is a companion letter to Colossians, and here we find the bracing instruction, taken perhaps from an early Christian poem or hymn; "Awake, sleeper, rise from the dead, and the messiah will give you light!" (5:14).[116]

A. Skevington Wood sees this passage as referring to the resurrection from a state of sleep and death. He also sees connection in the resurrection as associated with baptism.

> The most likely solution seems to be that this is an early baptismal hymn based on Isaiah 60:1. The rhythm may have been borrowed from the mystery religions and consecrated to a Christian use. Paul is soon to mention hymns in the context of worship (v. 19). This may well have been a liturgical chant addressed to those about to be baptized.

> The exhortations "wake up" (*egeire*) and "rise from the dead" (*anasta ek ton nekron*) place the hymn firmly in context of resurrection. It might have been designed for use on Easter day. The connection between resurrection and baptism is so close that there is no need to restrict the intention. Moreover, in the primitive church baptism was described as an enlightenment (*photoismos*), a usage that may underlie Hebrews 6:4 and 10:32. The verb translated "shine" (*epiphaino*) is applied to the rising of a heavenly body and to the dawn of the day. Christ, as the morning star, has already risen and sheds his light on all who are raised to newness of life in him.[117]

JAIRUS' DAUGHTER

In the case of Jairus' twelve-year old daughter in Luke 8:41 – 56, we find that the daughter had died while Jesus was on the way to his house. Upon arrival at the home of Jairus, Jesus made a statement to the professional mourners assembled there. "Stop weeping, for she has not died, but is asleep."

The hired mourners knew that she was dead. They knew how to take a pulse back then too and everyone knew she was dead. In fact, at Jesus' statement that 'she is asleep,'" they broke into laughter at him, which also betrayed the lack of genuine mournfulness among these paid wailers.

Immediately Jesus "took her by the hand and called saying, 'Child, arise!' and her spirit (*pneuma, the rational soul*) returned."

---

[116] *N.T. Wright, Surprised By Hope. (New York, Harper Collins Publishers, 2008), 252.*
[117] *A. Skevington Wood, Ephesians From The Expositor's Bible Commentary, Volume 11. General Editor, Frank E. Gaebelein. (Grand Rapids, Zondervan Publishing House, 1984), 71.*

In this example Jesus exemplified the coming resurrection of all believers when he calls them back to life at the *parousia*. In the Old Testament Job also understood that his resurrection would come at the time that the Lord would call him back to life.

> Job 14:14 – 15 If a man dies, will he live again? All the days of my struggle I will wait until my change comes. You will call, and I will answer You; You will long for the work of Your hands.

It seems inescapable at this point that Jesus and the New Testament Scriptures present the dead as being "asleep." This would include full cessation of thought in the intermediate state. If the soul ceases to exist at death, since the soul is comprised of both the corpse and the spirit-breath of God in combination. Then when the spirit from God leaves the body, there is no longer life, there is no longer soul and there is therefore no longer thought, since the entirety of the living being, the soul, is dissolved into its basic component parts. These basic component parts consist of the dust of the earth and the breath of God (Genesis 2:7). The soul, or living being, and all mental comprehension, exists only as these elements are in perfectly united combination. Consequently, since the soul is not immortal, there is no former human being enjoying the beatific visions in heaven at this moment, nor, thankfully, is any soul in excruciating pain in hell at this instant, since they are all figuratively "asleep" in the grave awaiting the call of God at their appointed resurrection.

We must be careful to avoid the trap of accepting the immortality of the soul as it applies to those who are "asleep." If the soul is indeed mortal then there is absolutely no consciousness after death. In that condition of non-existence, the soul is not literally asleep in a living state. The soul is simply figuratively "asleep" until its revivification at the resurrection. This point is well made by Jon D. Levenson.

> Gevurot leaves open a question that readily occurs to us. What is the fate of the dead before they are resurrected? The identification of them as "those who sleep in the dust" tempts us to say that they are not really dead at all but only asleep, enfolded in God's protective grace until they are at last revived. The temptation is best resisted. For neither in the Hebrew Bible nor in rabbinic literature is sleep generally seen as such a benign state. It is more than occasionally associated with death, as it is here, just as waking up is associated (in both literatures) with resurrection. And "dust," not a pleasant place to sleep under the best of circumstances, recalls the Lord's sentence upon Adam that he shall:

> ...return to the ground –
> For from it you were taken.
> For dust you are,
> And to dust you shall return. (Gen 3:19)
>
> But neither should we say that the Gevurot benediction relegates the dead to oblivion until the day of their restoration into life. For they do still exist at least in the mind of God who faithfully remembers his promises to them and will bring about their redemption.[118]

In Luke 20, when Jesus was questioned by the Sadducees, who did not believe in the resurrection (that is why they were "sad you see"), the Lord made it plain that in God's eyes, even though they were physically dead, that all still exist in his eyes. The clear implication being that all will once again live before him in the resurrection. His intonation is not regarding a resurrection that takes place immediately upon death, but of the restoration to life that will take place "in the resurrection (vs. 33 – 36)" in the eschatonal sense.

> Luke 20:37 – 38 "But that the dead are raised, even Moses showed, in the passage about the burning bush, where he calls the Lord the God of Abraham and the God of Isaac, and the God of Jacob. Now He is not the God of the dead but of the living; for all live to Him."

Jesus made a plain statement to Nicodemus in John 3:13. Regarding that spiritual conversation he and Nicodemus were having, Jesus attempted to convey understanding regarding the state of the dead. This point is largely overlooked in the church today but it is nevertheless biblical and authoritative.

> If I told you earthly things and you do not believe, how will you believe if I tell you heavenly things? No one has ascended into heaven, but He who descended from heaven; the Son of Man.

Jesus' favorite appellation for himself was "Son of man." As a result we have no doubt that he was referring to himself as the only human who had ever been in heaven. He also clarified the matter of where righteous King David of Israel is today through the inspired preaching of Peter on the day of Pentecost in Acts 2:34 – 35.

> For it was not David who ascended into heaven, but he himself says: 'The Lord said to my Lord, "Sit at My right hand, until I make your enemies a footstool for your feet."'

---

[118] *Jon D. Levenson, Resurrection And The Restoration Of Israel. (New Haven, Yale University Press, 2006), 5 – 6.*

In this quotation of Psalm 110:1, the Holy Spirit assures us that David was told to patiently await the time of his vindication. In addition Jesus assures us that David is not a resident of heaven. If righteous King David, a man after God's own heart, is not in heaven, and Jesus said that "No man has ascended to heaven," then aren't we forced, as serious believers in the word of God, to believe Jesus and Scripture?

We have already dealt with the matters of tradition and the supposed carrying to heaven of Enoch and Elijah and found those traditional teachings to be wanting in terms of serious biblical scholarship. The matters of David and any human believer not being in heaven call into serious question our traditional belief.

JESUS AND THE THIEF ON THE CROSS

Another point of contention between the various viewpoints regarding the state of the dead is found in the matter of Jesus and the thief on the cross. The criminal had come to the point that he realized the genuine truth of Jesus' regal claims and asked to be remembered in that kingdom.

> Luke 23:42 – 43 And he was saying, "Jesus, remember me when You come in Your kingdom!" And He said to him, "Truly I say to you, today you shall be with Me in Paradise."

These verses are often used as a proof-text for the idea that the righteous dead go to heaven. Adam Clarke identifies himself as one of those as he denounces conditionalists who see it otherwise.

> This saying of our Lord is justly considered as a strong proof of the immateriality of the soul; and it is no wonder that those who have embraced the contrary opinion should endeavour to explain away this meaning. In order to do this, a comma is placed after today, and then our Lord is supposed to have meant, "Thou shalt be with me after the resurrection; I tell thee this, today." I am sorry to find men of great learning and abilities attempting to support this most feeble and worthless criticism. Such support a good cause cannot need; and, in my opinion, even a bad cause must be discredited by it.[119]

As a neophyte struggling Doctoral student, it is of some comfort to know that in Adam Clarke's eyes there are "men of great learning and abilities" who support the idea that Jesus had the eschaton in mind and not that very twenty-four hour day of their existence. Perhaps then this student is in good company.

---

[119] *Adam Clarke, Clarke's Commentary, Matthew – Revelation. (United States of America, Abingdon Press, 1977), 497.*

Robert H. Stein appears to be one of those "men of great learning and abilities" in that in his commentary he seems to support the idea that Jesus meant the kingdom age yet to come. He does not see Christ as intending that very twenty-four hour day of their being on the cross.

> To the criminal's vague "when" Jesus responded with a precise "today," *referring less to within the next twenty-four hours or before the sun goes down* than to *the realization of Jesus' reign through his death, resurrection, and ascension*. This day through Jesus' death, salvation was being achieved, and the criminal would share in it. As a result even though this took place temporally that day, "Luke's 'today' belongs...more to theology than to chronology."[120]

We must ask some important questions regarding theological perspectives on this issue. Neither logic nor Scripture seem to support popular belief regarding Jesus' statement to the criminal.

1. If paradise is intended to be heaven, and if Jesus ascended to paradise at his death along with the criminal, then why did Jesus of necessity ascend to his Father on the following Sunday, three days later? We see that imperative expressed in his conversation with Mary at the tomb on Sunday morning when Mary recognized her Lord.

> Jesus said to her, "Mary!" She turned and said to Him in Hebrew, "Rabboni!" (which means, Teacher). Jesus said to her, "Stop clinging to Me, for I have not yet ascended to the Father; but go to My brethren and say to them, 'I ascend to My Father and your Father, and My God and your God.'" (John 20:16-17)

Jesus found it necessary to ascend to present himself to the Father in heaven since, to this point, he had not been in heaven for the past three days. Neither had the criminal been in heaven for the past three days. We note in Scripture that on that very Sunday evening Jesus appeared to his disciples. They also clung to him but they did not receive the rebuke as did Mary. Therefore we are left to conclude that in the meantime, during the day on Sunday between those two meetings, that Jesus had indeed made his presentation of himself to his Father in heaven. This was the first presentation of himself to the Father in heaven after his crucifixion. Therefore he certainly had not been in heaven for the intervening three days while in the tomb.

2. If Jesus had descended to hell on that day and preached to souls suffering in hell-fire, as some believe (I Peter 3:18 – 20 & 4:6), then how could

---

[120] *Robert H. Stein, Luke, from The New American Commentary, Volume 24. General Editor, David S. Dockery. (Nashville, Broadman Press, 1992), 593.*

Jesus justifiably promise the criminal that he would be with Him in paradise on that day? If Jesus were instead in hell for the time his body was in the tomb it is inconceivable that the criminal would want to be there with him or that such a place could be considered a paradise.

The main point of Jesus' conversation with the criminal seems to be that salvation is immediately available to us today. Jesus' atoning sacrifice on the cross makes possible salvation for the criminal, even while they both were on the cross. Salvation is available to all who heed and respond to the call of God today.

Another major consideration is that of the mental awareness of the criminal while in a state of death. As explained before, the dead know nothing, according to Scripture, and our reawakening to life occurs at the resurrection at the eschaton. The criminal will be unaware of the passage of time from his death to his resurrection. In that sense it will seem to him as if his next moment of consciousness will be in the paradisical presence of Jesus on the very same day of his death.

As Adam Clarke points out so eloquently, the conditionalist sees that in the translation of the Greek, where there is no punctuation, a proper English translation would put the comma after "today" rather than before. In this case the comma placement is truly in the hands of the translator and his particular doctrinal position and bias. If the comma were placed after "today," then this ambiguous mystery would be much better and more clearly stated. "Truly I say to you today, you shall be with Me in Paradise."

Odom likewise demonstrates the proper placement of the comma. Of particular interest is his assertion that after three days in the tomb that Jesus had not yet ascended to heaven (paradise).

> The translators, supposing that men go either to heaven or to torment immediately after death, inserted a comma before the word "today," so as to make Jesus say it that way. This is obviously an error. Christ did not go to heaven on the day He died. When He appeared to Mary Magdalene the morning of His resurrection, which was the third day after His death, "Jesus saith unto her, Touch me not; for *I am not yet ascended to my Father.*" John 20:17. So on Sunday morning the Saviour had not yet ascended to heaven.
>
> Joseph B. Rotherham, in the emphasized New Testament, renders this passage in these words: "Verily I say unto thee this day: With Me shalt thou be in Paradise." Luke 23:43. And George M. Lamsa, in his translation of the New Testament from Aramaic sources, renders it as follows: "Truly I say to you today, You will be with Me in Paradise."[121]

[121] Robert Leo Odom, *Is Your Soul Immortal?* (Ukiah, CA., Orion Publishing, 2007), 94 – 95.

Paul At Home With The Lord

Essentially the same can be said of the statement by Paul in 2 Corinthians 5:6 – 8. This statement too is used as a proof-text for the heavenly destiny of believers at the moment of their death.

> We are of good courage, I say, and prefer rather to be absent from the body and to be at home with the Lord.

It seems impossible to recount the innumerable times that this writer has heard popular evangelical preachers roll this verse off of their silver tongues while promoting the idea that Christians go to heaven upon death. In this examination, it is apparent that we must keep all of Paul's theology in mind when considering his statement.

First, let's examine Paul's theological basis. He was a Hebrew of the Hebrews and studied under the greatest teacher of Judaism of his day, Gamaliel. Old Testament Scripture, as we have already discovered, taught the resurrection of the dead at the end of this age. Jesus' friend Martha displayed her understanding of the Old Testament Scriptures in that regard when she retorted to his assertion that her brother Lazarus would rise again.

> "I know that he will rise again in the resurrection on the last day"
> John 11:24

As a learned pharisaic Israelite, Paul knew that concept as well. In fact, in his writings he believed in and focuses our attention on the resurrection rather than on the concept of immediate acceptance into heaven. In Philippians 3:10 – 11 Paul demonstrates that point.

> That I may know Him and the power of His resurrection and the fellowship of His sufferings, being conformed to His death; in order that I may attain to the resurrection from the dead.

No New Testament writer is as eloquent nor as verbose regarding his attention to our hope in the resurrection as is Paul. He proves that point in his statements regarding the coming of Christ with its associated resurrection of believers in both I Corinthians 15:50 – 58 and also in I Thessalonians 4:13 – 18. Therein he also describes the state of the dead as being "asleep" until the coming of Jesus.

In regards to Paul's theology, that the dead are metaphorically asleep in the grave until the resurrection at Jesus' second coming, we must note what he says regarding the intermediate state. In I Corinthians 15:18 he speaks of the uselessness of our faith in Christ if there is no resurrection.

> Then those who have fallen asleep in Christ have perished.

But why would Paul even bother speaking of the state of dead believers, those in Christ, needing the resurrection if they had already been granted eternal life in heaven after their physical death? If their eternal and immortal souls are now in heaven, then the resurrection would be of no value and in fact would be a totally superfluous event. Paul's theology clearly would not accept our traditional Christian teaching on heaven, hell, purgatory or any other considerations of the intermediate state. He would only agree that the souls of dead believers would be non-existent and "asleep" until the much awaited resurrection. He tells us that we will not be resurrected to life until the second advent.

> I Corinthians 15:23 But each in his own order: Christ the first fruits, after that those who are Christ's at his coming.

The concept of conscious life in an intermediate state is also opposed by Paul Althaus. He demonstrates that the acceptance of the concept of the immortality of the soul makes necessary the consideration of the intermediate state as a condition in which the life of the soul continues. He sees such a concept as creating many problems for Christian Theology.

> Another recent critic of the doctrine of the intermediate state is Paul Althaus, a Lutheran theologian (1888 – 1966). This doctrine, he maintains, is to be rejected since it presupposes the independent continued existence of a bodiless soul, and is therefore tinged with Platonism. Althaus advances a number of objections to the doctrine of the intermediate state. This doctrine does not do justice to the seriousness of death, since the soul seems to pass through death unscathed. By holding that without the body man can be totally blessed and totally happy, this doctrine denies the significance of the body. The doctrine empties the resurrection of its meaning; the more one fills up the blessedness of the individual after death, the more one detracts from the significance of the last day. If, according to this doctrine, believers after death are already blessed and the wicked are already in hell, why is the day of judgment still necessary? The doctrine of the intermediate state is thoroughly individualistic; it involves a private kind of blessedness rather than fellowship with others, and ignores the redemption of the cosmos, the coming of the kingdom, and the perfection of the church. In short, Althaus concludes, this doctrine rips apart what belongs together; soul and body, the individual and the community, blessedness and final glory, the destiny of individuals and the destiny of the world.[122]

As the thief on the cross would be unaware of the passage of time while asleep and without mental ability in the grave, because of his soul's

---

[122] Anthony A. Hoekema, *The Bible and the Future*. (Grand Rapids, William B. Eerdmans Publishing Co., 1994), 93 – 94.

nonexistence, so also did Paul understand that he too would not be aware of time and that in his next moment of consciousness he would indeed "be at home with the Lord." Consequently there is no authority for 2 Corinthians 5:8 being a proof-text on Christians ascending to heaven at the moment of death.

Lazarus And The Rich Man

In Luke 16:19 – 31 we see the parable of the rich man and Lazarus. This passage is often used as a proof-text demonstrating that people either go to heaven or hell upon death. Charles Ryrie is no exception and he explains his views in his Study Bible:

> *In Hades*, The unseen world in general, but specifically here the abode of the unsaved dead between death and judgment at the great white throne. In this saying the Lord taught (1) conscious existence after death, (2) the reality and torment of hell, (3) no second chance after death, and (4) the impossibility of the dead communicating with the living. The two men in this story illustrate two different lives, two different deaths, and two different destinies.[123]

On the other hand, it is difficult to find a modern day expositor who is willing to state agreement with Ryrie's position. Of the seven major multi-volume commentaries in my possession, all of them refer to this text as a parable and deny that it represents any historical reality. Robert H. Stein offers this regarding the nature of the story.

> Luke, however, clearly thought this was a parable, for he introduced it with "There was a (certain) rich man". In all but one this was used to introduce a parable (10:30; 14:16; 15:11; 16:1 [rich is added]; 16:19 [rich is added]; 19:12 ["of noble birth" is added]). The last six examples are furthermore all introduced by "he [Jesus] said/was saying" whereas 14:2 is clearly part of a narrative. This account also begins with the same introduction as the parable in 19:1, "There was a rich man," so that Luke intended for his readers to interpret this as a parable, not as a historical account.[124]

Michael Feazell offers two powerful reasons for Jesus telling this story. In addition he emphasizes the reason why only one scriptural witness is not enough to form a biblical doctrine.

---

[123] *Charles Caldwell Ryrie, Th.D., Ph.D., Ryrie Study Bible, Expanded Edition. (Chicago, Moody Press, 1995), 1655 – 1656.*
[124] *Robert H. Stein, Luke, from The New American Commentary, Volume 24. General Editor, David S. Dockery. (Nashville, Broadman Press, 1992), 422.*

Have you ever heard that God is incapable of reaching those who do not become believers before they die? It's a cruel and destructive doctrine, and its so-called "proof" is a single verse in the parable known as Lazarus and the Rich Man. But like all of Scripture, the parable of Lazarus and the Rich Man falls within a particular context and needs to be understood in that context.

It is always bad business to base a doctrine on one verse alone, and especially on a verse in a story designed to make a different point altogether. Jesus told the parable of Lazarus and the Rich Man for two reasons: 1) to expose and condemn the refusal of the leaders of Israel to believe in him, and 2) to reverse common assumptions about riches being a sign of God's favor and poverty being proof of God's disfavor.[125]

David Wenham also sees this as a parable without a historical basis. He discerns no intention of Jesus to convey a picture of the after-life but rather as a convenient vehicle to teach of one's responsibility regarding the seriousness and reality of the coming judgment.

However, even to try to explain the parable in terms of Jewish speculative thinking about the geography and chronology of the after-life is probably a mistake. Jesus shows no interest in such speculation, in this parable or elsewhere. The parable was not intended as a map of the after-life, though it has often been used or misused in that way, but was meant to make some very clear points about getting into the coming feast of the kingdom of God, or rather about the dangers of not getting in, and about the fearfulness and irrevocability of judgment.[126]

In addition, Michael Feazell also goes on to illustrate that Jesus did not use this parable as an opportunity to accurately describe the state of the soul after death. He sees traditional theology as missing the point of the parable.

Jesus did not tell this parable to paint us a portrait of heaven and hell. It is a parable of judgment against the unbelieving religious leadership of the time, and unkind, selfish rich people of all times. Jesus uses the common Jewish imagery of the afterlife (that of Hades for the wicked and "being with Abraham" for the righteous) as a literary backdrop to make the point. In this parable Jesus was not commenting on the validity or accuracy of Jewish imagery of the afterlife; he was simply using that imagery as scenery for his story.

---

[125] Michael Feazell, *Lazarus and the Rich Man: A Tale of Unbelief.* Christian Odyssey, February – March, 2011. 12.

[126] David Wenham, The Parables of Jesus. (Downers Grove, Intervarsity Press, 1989), 145.

> Jesus' focus was not to satisfy our itching curiosities about what heaven and hell are like. His priority is to let us in on God's secrets (Romans 16:25; Ephesians 1:9, etc.), the mystery of the ages (Ephesians 3:4-5) – that in him, Jesus Christ, the Son of God incarnate, God has always been reconciling the world to himself (2 Corinthians 5:19).
>
> Our preoccupation with the details of the afterlife can only lead us away from the very point missed by the rich man in the story: Believe in the One who came back from the dead.[127]

Jesus did not design this parable to convey accurate information regarding the afterlife for either the righteous or the unrighteous. He simply was using an aspect of the folklore of his day to teach an important lesson about the seriousness of the call and expectations of God as related to salvation as well as the five brothers and their responsibility to hear and obey the word of God on their own.

Clark Pinnock understands the local color and imagery Jesus employed in this parable. Likewise he understands that current day popular preaching from this text is often unfairly used to describe the unending everlasting sufferings of hell.

> What about the text in the famous parable of the six brothers, in which Jesus describes a rich man suffering in hellish torments? Certainly the figure is there in the midst of much contemporary Jewish imagery and folklore. In a classic reversal-of-fortunes parable, the poor man is carried by the angels to Abraham's bosom. But unless there is a lot of room in the patriarch's lap, the detail seems to be imagery rather than a literal description of what the future life will actually be like. In addition, the story refers to *hades* (the intermediate state between death and resurrection), not to *gehenna* (the final end of the wicked), and is not strictly relevant to our subject. Nevertheless, the passage is regularly and unfairly appealed to in traditionalist literature to describe hell, not the intermediate state. The fact is that we cannot deduce from it what the final end of the wicked will be, apart from the issue of its literary genre.[128]

George Eldon Ladd also joins the discussion in seeing the parabolic nature of the story. He notes the confusing message conveyed if indeed it were of an actual historic event.

---

[127] Michael Feazell, *Lazarus and the Rich Man: A Tale of Unbelief. Christian Odyssey*, February – March 2011. 13.
[128] Clarke Pinnock, *Four Views On Hell, From Chapter Four, The Conditional View*. General Editor, William Crockett. (Grand Rapids, Zondervan Publishing, 1996), 156 – 157.

> The parable of the rich man and Lazarus has often been taken as a didactic passage to teach explicitly the state of the dead. This, however, is very difficult, for if this is a didactic passage, it teaches something contrary to the rest of Jesus' teaching, that wealth merits hades, and that poverty itself is rewarded in Paradise. This parable is no commentary on contemporary social life, nor does it intend to give teaching about the afterlife. It is really not a parable about the rich man and Lazarus, but about the five brothers. Jesus used contemporary folk-material to set forth the single truth that if people do not hear the word of God, a miracle such as a resurrection would not convince them.[129]

Even the witness of the Morning Star of the Reformation, John Wycliffe, saw this passage as a parable. He understood that no serious use of it should be made to define the actual state of the dead.

> In his exposition of Luke 16:19 – 31 – on the "parable" of the rich Man and Lazarus, as he termed it – he refused to base any doctrinal view on the parable, maintaining that it simply had a practical bearing on the duties of daily life.[130]

Hans Urs Von Balthasar sees this passage as a parable. He also believes it is meant to give us a rather simple and limited altruistic message.

> That the Parable of the Rich Glutton and the Poor Lazarus is not meant as anything more than an earnest warning to the living to have mercy on the beggar at their door is clear.[131]

We must consider that this passage cannot legitimately be used as a proof-text to demonstrate that the righteous go to heaven and the unsaved go to hell upon death. Indeed, Luke is the only Gospel writer who preserves the parable and there cannot be a legitimate establishment of doctrine without at least two or three supporting Scripture witnesses. Standing on it's own, this is only an interesting story, a parable that was largely aimed at the Pharisees and their religious peers who saw their wealth as a sign of righteousness.

---

[129] George Eldon Ladd, *A Theology of the New Testament*. (Grand Rapids, William B. Eerdmans Publishing Co., 1993), 194 – 195.
[130] Le Roy Edwin Froom, *The Conditionalist Faith of Our Fathers, Volume 2*. (Washington, D.C., Review and Herald Publishing Association, 1965), 59.
[131] Hans Urs Von Balthasar, *Dare We Hope "That All Men Be Saved"?* (San Francisco, Ignatius Press, 1988), 198.

The Reformers

Conditional Immortality depends on the biblical stand of the mortality of the soul and its metaphorical sleep or nonexistence during what is referred to as the intermediate state. Consequently, we will now look at the stance of three of the major members of the Protestant Reformation and the effect they had on this matter of the composition of the soul and of its condition during the intermediate state.

Among the reformers of the fourteenth through the sixteenth centuries, there are several outstanding names who were forefront in the Reformation of traditional Christianity, who also espoused the dormancy or sleep of the soul. Chief among them were John Wycliffe, Martin Luther and William Tyndale. These all saw the soul as sleeping during the intermediate state. Wycliffe, since he was the pioneer of the perspective and lacking the fuller understanding which developed later over time, retained an acceptance of the soul still being alive during that sleep because of his inherited view of the immortality of the soul from the church. We also discover that both Luther and Tyndale retained the later Psychopannychist position that the soul was alive during that dormancy. However, it seems that both Luther and Tyndale ultimately came to deny the immortality of the soul. We shall see this illustrated in Luther's reply to the papal bull of *Exsurge Domini*, of June 15, 1520 and in the case of Tyndale in statements he made later in life.

John Wycliffe

John Wycliffe is known as "the Morning Star of the Reformation" as he was the first individual of any significance who began to voice the changing perspectives of Protestantism after the religious ignorance that dominated the dark ages. Wycliffe was the most influential Christian personage of the fourteenth century who had served in various areas of responsibility including that of an instructor at Oxford, chaplain to the king and adviser to parliament. It was Wycliffe who translated the first English version of the Bible. His academic acumen was well attested to by all who knew him.

> Wyclif's knowledge of philosophy enabled him to expose its errors with devastating logic. And his skill in civil and ecclesiastical law prepared him to champion not only religious liberty for all but the civil rights of the crown, and to deny the papal claim of authority over civil rulers. Understanding the tactics of the schoolmen, he was in a position to counter them through his learning and to command the respect of foe, as well as friend. His championship of neglected and forgotten truths consequently compelled a hearing by the leading minds of the nation. Enemies could not cast

contempt upon the causes he championed and the positions he espoused by charging either ignorance or weakness. He was acknowledged by all as an intellectual giant.[132]

Wycliffe opposed prayers for the dead and the Roman doctrine of Purgatory. He called these teachings "pious lies" since he believed strongly that the soul was in a state of unconscious sleep between the time of one's death and the resurrection.

> Though he still believed in the separate existence of the soul, he taught that the state between death and the resurrection is that of sleep. Moreover, he held that the judgment of rewards would not take place until after the resurrection. Furthermore, he believed that the "greatest part" of the reward of the righteous would be "immortalitie or undedlynesses," received at the resurrection. That was indeed revolutionary for his day. He was distinctly a pioneer in advocating the "sleep of the soul" during death. This is brought out forcefully in *The Church and Her Members*, where he again maintains that the souls in "purgatory" are "dead," and cannot be benefited by prayers, hence were "clepid sleping ["called sleeping"]" or "slepen in purgatorye." It was a long stride out of the darkness of medieval theology.[133]

So we see that John Wycliffe, the earliest of the Protestant Reformers and the *Morning Star* of the Protestant Reformation, was clearly in the camp of those who understood from Scripture that men "slept" during the intermediate state and that they were neither in heaven, purgatory nor in hell in everlasting suffering and pain.

MARTIN LUTHER

The reformers of the medieval Church began with certain erroneous doctrinal traditions that were already extant in the church for generations before them. When it comes to presenting and preserving scriptural truth to a church that is already in a confused state of having accepted pagan influence and teaching, the biggest problem is to first eliminate error in order that finally biblical truth can be taught and accepted. Martin Luther and the other reformers demonstrated gradual change from previous dogma and that change came slowly but surely with Luther.

---

[132] *Le Roy Edwin Froom, The Conditionalist Faith of Our Fathers, Volume 2. (Washington, D.C., Review and Herald Publishing Association, 1965), 51.*
[133] *Ibid, 59.*

Ray Anderson speaks of the errors in philosophy that were strongly attached to the period of the reformation. He notes that the immortality of the soul was such a strong part of church teaching that it actually became official doctrine of the church by the Lateran Council of 1512.

> Yet, there is within the Christian tradition a persistent teaching that the soul of human persons possesses some kind of immortality by nature. It has been widely accepted that the neo-platonic emphasis on a body-soul dualism, with immortality attributed to the soul, had significant influence in early patristic theology. As a result, there existed in the medieval Church a strong belief in the immortality of the soul. The doctrine of the immortality of the soul was declared official dogma by the Lateran Council of 1512, and was accepted in principle by the Protestant Reformers.[134]

PSYCHOPANNYCHIST TO THNETOPSYCHIST

In spite of the fact that Martin Luther began his career as a Roman Catholic priest, and initially accepted church teaching on the immortality of the soul, Luther is to be accounted among those who, over time, later understood the soul to sleep while in the intermediate state. He was among the Psychopannychists of his day who believed that the soul lives after the death of the body but that it is unconscious until the General Resurrection. Gradually Luther later came to change his mind about the immortality of the soul, having become of the Thnetopsychist persuasion by the time he issued his response to the Pope on his teachings. In his response to the papal bull *Exsurge Domini*, of June 15, 1520, which condemned forty-one of his propositions, Luther spoke of the teaching of the immortality of the soul as being one of the Pope's "monstrous opinions."

> With ironical permission Luther grants to the pope the right and power to make special "articles of faith" for himself and his own followers. He lists five in the series, including the "immortality of the soul" as the fifth, all and each of which Luther expressly rejects. The significance of including "'*the soul is immortal* ["*animam esse immortalem*"]" in what he denominates "monstrous opinions" and "Roman corruptions," is, of course, obvious. And he added immediately that these "all" came out of the "Roman dunghill of decretals'" – thus harking back to the pope's bull of December 19, 1513, wherein he declared the natural immortality of the soul to be a doctrine of the Catholic Church. Here are Luther's exact words:

---

[134] *Ray S. Anderson, Theology, Death And Dying. (New York, Basil Blackwell Inc., 1986), 57 – 58.*

> "But I permit the Pope to make articles of faith for himself and his faithful, such as [1] *The Bread and wine are transubstantiated in the sacrament. [2] The essence of God neither generates, nor is generated. [3] The soul is the substantial form of the human body. [4] The Pope is the emperor of the world, and the king of heaven, and God upon earth.* [5] THE SOUL IS IMMORTAL, with all those monstrous opinions to be found in the Roman dunghill of decretals."[135]

One may get the idea that perhaps Luther was pushed over the edge by the constant opposition that he faced from Rome and that he came to the point that he also rejected the immortality of the soul and became of the Thnetopsychist opinion. In the end he cast the concept of the immortality of the soul upon *the Roman dunghill of decretals*.

Archbishop Blackburn had studied and summarized Luther's position for us. In his summation, Blackburne states:

> Luther espoused the doctrine of the sleep of the soul, upon a scripture foundation, and then he made use of it as a confutation of purgatory and saint worship, and continued in that belief to the last moment of his life.

> Blackburne then adds that Luther's commentary on *Ecclesiastes*, published in 1532, was "clearly and indisputably on the side of those who maintain the sleep of the soul." Blackburne, the Anglican scholar, is cited here because, having studied deeply into Luther's position nearly two centuries previously, and having searched out all the pertinent source evidences bearing thereon, he recorded this definite opinion: "Luther mentioned the *immortality of the soul, as* a portentous opinion, *supported by nothing but the Pope's decrees.*"[136]

Those who understood the biblical position regarding the state of the dead to be one of unconscious sleep included both the Psychopannychists and the Thnetopsychists. The Psychopannychists made allowance for the traditional belief of the immortality of the soul while the Thnetopsychists did not. The Thnetopsychists held that the human soul is similar to that of animals and that the souls (or lives) of both perish with the body.[137]

---

[135] *Le Roy Edwin Froom, The Conditionalist Faith of Our Fathers, Volume 2. (Washington, D.C., Review and Herald Publishing Association, 1965), 73.*
[136] *Ibid, 74.*
[137] *Norman T. Burns, Christian Mortalism from Tyndale to Milton. (Cambridge, Harvard University Press, 1972), 17.*

> The psychopannychists believed that the immortal substance called soul literally slept until the resurrection of the body, the thnetopsychists, denying that the soul was an immortal substance, believed that the soul slept after death only in a figurative sense. Both groups of soul sleepers believed in the personal immortality of the individual after the resurrection of the body, and so they should not be confused with the annihilationists.[138]

The Oxford English Dictionary defines the terms as they emerge from their Greek source words. *Psychopannychy* or *psychopannychism* derive from *psuche* and *pannuchios*. *Psychopannychism* is defined as "all-night sleep of the soul", the state in which "the soul sleeps between death and the day of judgment". Thnetopsychism, is formed after the Greek *thnetos* and *psuche*, as "the doctrine…that the soul dies with the body, and is recalled to life with it at the Day of Judgment".[139]

Luther's perspective gave him opportunity to use his initial *psychopannychist* belief in opposition to the practices of Rome, which emphasized prayers for the dead and the payment of indulgences to speed their departure from purgatory. As Burns says: "Martin Luther used psychopannychism to bar the gate against Rome's practices."[140]

Sola Scriptura

In Luther's view, Scripture must take predominance over philosophy. Thus, it is no surprise that one of the battle cries of himself and other reformers was *"sola Scriptura"*. Burns expresses the apparent views of Luther when he writes of a papal order requiring his submission to traditional papal authority and interpretation of doctrine.

> When, in 1520, he answered the bull ordering him to submit to papal authority, Luther expressed his impatience with the Roman habit of basing the doctrines of immortality on philosophy as if Holy Scripture were not a sufficient guide…Although the passage (quoted from Luther's response) does not make clear exactly what Luther's attitude toward the dogma of immortality is, it is certain that he considers the elements drawn out of Aristotle to be irrelevant to, and probably contrary to, Christ's teaching.[141]

---

[138] Norman T. Burns, *Christian Mortalism from Tyndale to Milton*. (Cambridge, Harvard University Press, 1972), 17.
[139] Bryan W. Ball, *The Soul Sleepers, Christian Mortalism from Wycliffe to Priestley*. (Cambridge, James Clarke & Co., 2008), 20.
[140] Norman T. Burns, *Christian Mortalism from Tyndale to Milton*. (Cambridge, Harvard University Press, 1972), 27
[141] Ibid. 28 – 29.

Several years ago, having entered into an amicable discussion of the state of the dead with a pastor in my area, after an hour or so of discussion he looked at me and stated, "Your position is correct. I just like to make people feel good when I conduct a funeral and so I simply tell them that their loved one is in heaven."

Ray S. Anderson emphasizes how Ernest Becker sees such an approach as being spiritually unhealthy. To use such unbiblical reasoning diminishes the real value of human existence and anthropological theology.

> In his psychologizing of death for the sake of creating a valid philosophy of life, Becker has thought about death more honestly and patiently than most of our contemporaries. His critique stands as a warning to the bastions of materialism and scientism that the human spirit will not yield to a definition of death which makes it only a matter of clinical concern at the end of life. At the same time, he has exposed the superficiality and downright unhealthiness of religious attempts to conceal the reality of death by promising immortality 'in the sweet bye and bye'.[142]

Perhaps the pastor I spoke with, regarding the nature of the soul and salvation, would have benefited from reading Martin Luther's prescribed funeral service. In it he describes death as a "deep, strong, sweet sleep."

> But we Christians, who have been redeemed from all this through the precious blood of God's Son, should train and accustom ourselves in faith to despise death and regard it as a deep, strong, sweet sleep; to consider the coffin as nothing other than our Lord Jesus' bosom or Paradise, the grave as nothing other than a soft couch of ease or rest. As verily, before God, it truly is just this; for he testifies, John 11:21: Lazarus, our friend sleeps; Matthew 9:24: The maiden is not dead, she sleeps.
>
> This, too, St. Paul in 1 Corinthians 15, removes from sight all hateful aspects of death as related to our mortal body and brings forward nothing but charming and joyful aspects of the promised life. He says there (vv. 42 ff.): It is sown in corruption and will rise in incorruption; it is sown in dishonor (that is, a hateful, shameful form) and will rise in glory; it is sown in weakness and will rise in strength; it is sown a natural body and will rise a spiritual body.[143]

In this study of the beliefs of Martin Luther, it becomes rather obvious that Luther's views changed over time to include full rejection of the concept

---

[142] *Ray S. Anderson, Theology, Death And Dying. (New York, Basil Blackwell Inc., 1986), 31.*
[143] *Le Roy Edwin Froom, The Conditionalist Faith of Our Fathers, Volume 2. (Washington, D.C., Review and Herald Publishing Association, 1965), 77.*

of the immortality of the soul. Martin Luther was one of the primary movers in the advancement of Thnetopsychism in his day.

John Calvin

At the same time another important reformer, by the name of John Calvin, launched a campaign against the whole idea of mortalism and psychopannychism. He maintained the church's traditional stance on the immortality of the soul and did not express any difference with the Roman Church on these issues. He supported efforts to spurn, and stigmatize the leading figures of the Protestant Reformation for their apparent "heresy" regarding the makeup and state of the soul.

> Calvin, of course, was not of the same mind at all. He saw mortalism in any form as heresy, and a threat to the order he sought to bring to the Reformation and to the reformed church which he was in the process of shaping and which he fervently hoped would endure into the future. He called mortalists, particularly psychopannychists, "Babblers" and "Hypnologists", and mortalists in general soul-killers, "*psuchoktonoi*, assassins of the soul". Calvin clung to the traditional, prevailing view of immortality, believing in the soul's separate existence and its continuing consciousness after death.[144]

Modern day Lutheranism is a far cry from the beliefs of Martin Luther in the sixteenth century because of the influence of John Calvin on the Protestant Reformation. Edward Fudge identifies one of the reasons why Luther's views did not prevail even in the church which derives its name from him. Fudge identifies a major problem in that regard which was John Calvin's teachings on the immortality of the soul. Calvin rejected the sleep of the soul and instead held the traditional belief in immortality of the soul and the soul's presence in either heaven or hell at death. In order to maintain peace between himself and his fellow Protestant reformer, Luther soft-pedaled his position on soul sleep. As a consequence, the louder voice of Calvin eventually won the day and his views on the intermediate state became the prominent teaching even in Lutheranism.

> Although Calvin and Luther differed on the soul's state after death, Calvin's intense zeal outweighed Luther's depth of commitment. It is the distinct contribution of Burns that he has detailed the way in which Luther's opinion was conceded in the interests of Reformed unity, its defense passing to the hated Anabaptists. As a result,

---

[144] Bryan W. Ball, *The Soul Sleepers, Christian Mortalism from Wycliffe to Priestley.* (Cambridge, James Clarke & Co., 2008), 39.

Calvin's view became first and dominant and finally the orthodox doctrine of most established Protestant churches.[145]

As mentioned in the above quote by Fudge, Norman T. Burns preserves the fact that the Lutheran reformers did not press for Luther's Thnetopsychistic views regarding the nature of the mortal soul and its sleep in the grave. Then with that theological vacuum in place, the position of Calvin was poised to take over the void in both Protestantism in general and in Lutheranism, specifically.

> When the Lutheran reformers failed to give vigorous support to psychopannychism, soul sleeping lost what small chance it might have had to be considered a debatable doctrine, a thing indifferent. Once it was identified solely with the Anabaptists, there was no hope for a hearing before respectable Protestants, ministers who believed God was reforming his Church but who did not want to be discharged from their livings, laymen who felt that not all of the Word of God had yet been clearly understood, but who were not prepared to attend irregular meetings and risk imprisonment and exile. Unchallenged by the doctrine of a Reformation church of comparable stature, the view of the churches of Geneva and Zurich (and of Rome) on the nature of the soul had to prevail in England.[146]

Christian Theology should not be afraid to examine honestly the differences between the reformers, theologians and religious leaders. It is healthy to be able to discover the truth of the historical nature of changes in thinking among those who were historically involved in determining the doctrinal positions of the church. To attempt to hide those differences is dishonest and presents a biased and inappropriately sanitized version of the truth of doctrinal formulation. Clark Pinnock recognizes that such dishonest practice obscures important aspects of the decision making process.

> Some readers may be initially surprised to learn that evangelical theology comes in different versions at all. They may have thought that there was just one uncontested set of convictions all real Christians have always held from the beginning. This is a common misunderstanding among us. Although there is a basic grammar of faith including belief in the triune God and the unique salvation in Jesus Christ, in other areas such as the outworking of God's saving purposes there has not been complete agreement.

---

[145] Edward William Fudge, *The First That Consumes, Revised Edition.* (Milton Keynes, UK., Patternoster Press, 1994), 37.
[146] Norman T. Burns, *Christian Mortalism from Tyndale to Milton.* (Cambridge, Harvard University Press, 1972), 32 – 33.

On the contrary, Luther's version of how God works salvation and relates to the world is distinctive and different in some respects from Wesley's and Augustine's versions. They represent different versions of the broad evangelical and Christian tradition. And the differences between them are worth debating and should not always be shoved underneath the rug in a show of unity. For some purposes it makes sense to call a wide variety of Christians "evangelicals" to distinguish them from liberal reductionists for example, but it can also be quite misleading to call them by this adjective if the umbrella term obscures important differences among them which should not be lost sight of.[147]

One does have to seriously wonder how perhaps the course of the Christian Church may have changed for the significant better if only Luther and his adherents had pressed more vigorously for his view on the mortality of the soul and its figurative metaphoric sleep in the intermediate state. It would have changed several traditional doctrinal positions of the church and made it much more Scripture based than the Hellenistic philosophic basis that prevails and persists to this day.

WILLIAM TYNDALE

Tyndale had been a follower of the teachings of Luther and was instrumental in translating and bringing the Bible to the general public in their own English tongue. For that forbidden practice and possibly because of his Mortalistic views, he was burned at the stake in the town of Vilvorde in A.D. 1536. At his execution he made one final cry for religious freedom when he shouted, "Lord! Open the king of England's Eyes."[148] A posthumous vindication of Tyndale came in 1611 at the release of the King James Version of the Bible. Tyndale's translation of the Scriptures amounted to ninety percent of the finished product.[149]

Tyndale believed that traditional Christian teaching of the doctrine of the immortality of the soul did great harm to the truth of Scripture. He also understood that it hampered the true belief of Christians and that it led to the diminishment and indeed, the destruction of the biblical focus on the resurrection.

Men like Tyndale, who believed that ideas of blissful immortality

---

[147] Clark H. Pinnock, General Editor, *The Grace Of God And The Will Of Man.* (Minneapolis, Bethany House Publishers, 1989), ix.
[148] *John Fox, Fox's Book of Martyrs. William Byron Forbush, D.D., Editor. (Grand Rapids, Zondervan Publishing House, 1978), 184.*
[149] Le Roy Edwin Froom, *The Conditionalist Faith of Our Fathers, Volume 2.* (Washington, D.C., Review and Herald Publishing Association, 1965), 91.

before the resurrection of the body threatened Christian belief in the promised drama of the conquest of death on the Last Day, were prepared to discover that soul sleeping is the doctrine of Scripture.[150]

In his *Answer to Sir Tomas More's Dialogue*, Tyndale made a defense as to the sleep of the souls and its being not only the doctrine of Luther but actually being the very teaching and doctrine of the Bible itself.

> And ye, in putting them [departed souls] in heaven, hell, and purgatory, destroy the arguments wherewith Christ and Paul prove the resurrection. What God doth with them, that shall we know when we come to them. The true faith putteth the resurrection, which we be warned to look for every hour. The heathen philosophers, denying that, did put that the souls did ever live. And the pope joineth the spiritual doctrine of Christ and the fleshly doctrine of philosophers together; things so contrary that they cannot agree, no more than the Spirit and the flesh do in a Christian man. And because the fleshly-minded pope consenteth unto heathen doctrine, therefore he corrupteth the scripture to stablish it....and again, if the souls be in heaven, tell me why they be not in as good case as the angels be? And then what cause is there of the resurrection?[151]

Tyndale was a student of prophecy and he came to the conclusion that the pope was the Antichrist. Along the way he had come to admire Luther's outspoken positions on natural immortality and Purgatory and they both had come to similar conclusions.

> It is significant that the two men – Luther and Tyndale – who spearheaded the Reformation in Germany and in England by translating the Bible into the vernacular of their respective peoples, should both be thus led to detect this distinctive Roman departure on the nature of man and the sleep of the soul, along with related Catholic innovations, both going on record against the Platonic philosophy that had established itself in Roman theology.[152]

Though Tyndale seemed to accept the concept of the immortality of the soul, he spent his writings focusing on the biblical resurrection at the end of the age. He saw such emphasis as being far more important than that of the soul's existence during the intermediate state.

---

[150] Norman T. Burns, *Christian Mortalism from Tyndale to Milton.* (Cambridge, Harvard University Press, 1972), 34.
[151] *Ibid*, 101.
[152] Le Roy Edwin Froom, *The Conditionalist Faith of Our Fathers, Volume 2.* (Washington, D.C., Review and Herald Publishing Association, 1965), 93 – 94

Both Frith and Tyndale, then, inclined toward the belief that the soul slept in the intermediate state, but neither felt that Scripture justified making an article of faith out of even so indefinite a doctrine as Psychopannychism. But if Tyndale was willing to consider the precise nature of the intermediate state a thing indifferent, he would not tolerate dogmatism on the subject from anyone else, particularly if the dogma threatened to make the resurrection of the body superfluous.[153]

An alternate view to the conscious immortality of the state of the dead was summed up in the term Mortalism. By its very name, this belief focused on the idea that the soul was mortal. Mortalism rejected traditional teaching on the immortality of the soul. Regarding that position, Thomas Edward wrote a popular book on heresy in 1646 in which he stated 267 concepts that he saw to be erroneous in the Christian teaching of his day. Of those 267 points he devoted eleven mentions to the errors of the doctrine of Mortalism. Among them, this writer found point number 173 and enjoyed it with some levity and amusement.

> 173. No man is yet in hell, neither shall any be there until the judgment; for God doth not hang first, and judge after.[154]

To this point we have seen that a number of the principle individuals responsible for the Protestant Reformation were also advocates of the soul sleep concept. In the case of Luther and Tyndale, it is also apparent that they ultimately came to or were approaching the Thnetopsychist camp. Luther more dramatically renounced the immortality of the soul and Tyndale was certainly moving in that direction before his unfortunate martyrdom, being burned at the stake at Brussels in Flanders on October 6, 1536 because of his "heresies." As the Pioneer in the movement, John Wycliffe had an understandably underdeveloped theology on the matter that the soul sleeps, and so we cannot say he was anything but an early Psychopannychist.

Conditional Immortality depends on the Thnetopsychist position, accepting only the mortality of the soul and the opportunity for all non-believers who were inadequately taught, or not instructed at all, the genuine gospel. It is biblically demonstrable that these will have a real first time opportunity for salvation at the white throne judgment period that follows the general resurrection of mankind. The concept of immortal souls in heaven, hell or purgatory in the intermediate state negates this doctrinal

---

[153] Norman T. Burns, *Christian Mortalism from Tyndale to Milton.* (Cambridge, Harvard University Press, 1972), 106.
[154] *Ibid,* 101.

stance. That is why this book is focused on drawing attention to the biblical position regarding both the mortality of the soul and its dissolution at death, which brings about the soul's (or life's) temporary non-existence and the metaphorical sleep we read of in Scripture.

In summary, chapter six shows that Jesus' teaching on the state of the dead indicates that they are "asleep" in the grave until the resurrection. He states this fact regarding both his friend Lazarus and Jairus' daughter. Also we have seen that the argument that the thief on the cross went to paradise "today" is demonstrably fallacious. Paul's hope was in the resurrection, not in instantly being sent to heaven upon death. The parable of Lazarus and the rich man is shown to be only a story of no actual historic reality and of no value as a proof-text for the position of believers going to heaven upon death. In chapter six we also saw that a number of the primary movers in the Protestant Reformation including John Wycliffe, Martin Luther and William Tyndale were of the persuasion that the dead were "asleep" in the grave until the resurrection.

Having laid the foundation of the nonexistence of those who are in a state of death, we are now ready to explore various viewpoints regarding hell fire. In chapter seven we will see the orthodox position of hell, questions as to its flames being unquenchable and the views of contemporary writers as well as those of Martin Luther on the subject.

Chapter Seven
Ever-Burning And Ever-Suffering In Hell-Fire?

Chapter Seven

Ever-Burning And Ever-Suffering In Hell Fire?

> I believe that unrepentant sinners perish,
> die the second death
> and are finally destroyed.[155]

Proponents of Conditional Immortality accept the possibility that most people may be saved. This is unlike Universalism, which sees that all people who have ever lived will accept salvation in Jesus Christ. Biblical statements indicate that there are those who will be consumed at the second death in the lake of fire. If some are consumed and destroyed in those flames then there certainly is no absolutely universal salvation. On the other hand, Scripture gives allowance for the possibility that most can see salvation.

When he was speaking of the final judgment, Jesus made it obvious that there are those who will be sent into eternal punishment. At this point we must understand that "punishment" does not equate with "punishing" as if the active infliction of painful punishment is on-going. Only the effect of punishment is on-going, that is that the punished one is no longer alive, is no longer existent, but has been consumed in the flames of the lake of fire and is no longer a living entity.

> Matthew 25:45 – 46 Then He will answer them, 'Truly I say to you, to the extent that you did not do it to one of the least of these, you did not do it to Me.' These will go away into eternal punishment, but the righteous into eternal life.

According to Rob Bell, the term "eternal punishment" used by Jesus in this passage does not indicate a never-ending eternity as we would understand the term. He explains that the Greek words Jesus used, *aion* of *kolazo*, indicate an age or a period of time of intense "pruning and trimming of the branches of a plant so it can flourish." *Kolazo* here is a horticultural term. In that intense pruning and trimming that takes place for a specified period of time the sentence could be translated "'a period of pruning' or 'a time of trimming.' Or an intense experience of correction."[156]

---

[155] Clark H. Pinnock, *Four Views Of Hell*. (Grand Rapids, Zondervan, 1996), 37.
[156] Rob Bell, *Love Wins. A Book About Heaven, Hell, And The Fate Of Every Person Who Ever Lived*. (New York, Harper One, 2011) 91.

Bell goes on to explain that the Hebrew term *olam* which is often translated as "forever" in the Old Testament is similar to the Greek *aion*. Both terms indicate a limited period of time.

> The closest the Hebrew writers come to a word for "forever" is the word *olam*. *Olam* can be translated as "to the vanishing point," "in the far distance," "a long time," "long lasting," or "that which is at or beyond the horizon." When *olam* refers to God, as in Psalm 90 ("from everlasting to everlasting you are God"), it's much closer to the word "forever" as we think of it, time without beginning or end. But then in the other passages, when it's not describing God, it has very different meanings, as when Jonah prays to God, who let him down into the belly of a fish "forever" (*olam*) and then, three days later, brought him out of the belly of the fish. (Jonah 2:6)
>
> *Olam*, in this instance, turns out to be three days. It's a versatile, pliable word, in most occurrences referring to a particular period of time.
>
> So when we read "eternal punishment," it's important that we don't read categories and concepts into a phrase that aren't there. Jesus isn't talking about forever as we think of forever.[157]

We must also note that this punishment in Matthew 25:46 is not stated to take place upon their original first death. This punishment is meted out after the general resurrection and the following judgment, which will result in the second and final death of the unsaved. The point is exhibited even more strongly in Revelation 20.

> Revelation 20:11 – 15 Then I saw a great white throne and Him who sat upon it, from whose presence earth and heaven fled away, and no place was found for them. And I saw the dead, the great and the small, standing before the throne and books were opened and another book was opened, which is the book of life; and the dead were judged from the things which were written in the books, according to their deeds. And the sea gave up the dead which were in it, and death and hades gave up the dead which were in them; and they were judged, every one of them according to their deeds. Then death and Hades were thrown into the lake of fire. This is the second death, the lake of fire. And if anyone's name was not found written in the book of life, he was thrown into the lake of fire.

It is an incredible thing to comprehend that those who are so clearly taught the way of salvation, first in the millennial timeframe and then later

---

[157] Rob Bell, *Love Wins. A Book About Heaven, Hell, And The Fate Of Every Person Who Ever Lived.* (New York, Harper One, 2011) 101.

after the general resurrection, preceding the white throne judgment, as to how some will still adamantly refuse to accept Jesus as Lord and Savior. Subsequently they will have been responsible for their own eternal destruction. Martin Luther spoke on this very matter during a sermon from John 15:17 – 25.

> So our heavenly Father would very much like for us to be saved and, therefore, has ordained for us, not eternal fire but heaven and eternal life. But we go on despising the forgiveness of sins through Christ as a trifling treasure. If only we had enough money and possessions! These mean more to us. Moreover, we also take no delight in doing what God tells us to do in order to serve Him. Since, then, we degenerate to the very level of the devil and observe his will more than the Word of our Lord God, it must follow that we are obliged to share this judgment. We prepare this doom for ourselves. We could, to be sure, have a better lot; but we do not want the better lot.[158]

In other words, Luther is saying that we are the arbiters of our own destiny. Salvation, or the lack thereof, is entirely in our hands, we are the decision makers. Unfortunately there are those who will, even in the final analysis, choose to neglect and refuse salvation in Christ.

We should take notice of a number of points in Revelation 20:11-15 which counter traditional Christian teaching on the subject of judgment and punishment.

1. The dead stand before God. There is no indication that they have been summoned either from heaven or from hell for this white throne judgment. They have simply been resurrected from the dead, just as the righteous were resurrected from the dead at the first resurrection (vs. 6). There also is no indication here that they had been in some state of immortal consciousness while in the intermediate state.
2. In verse 13 we see that the dead come up from two distinct places. The sea and from Hades. Those who died in the sea never had an opportunity to be buried in Hades, the grave. This demonstrates to us that Hades, in the biblical sense, only refers to the grave, not to some place of reserve for immortal souls who have some state of consciousness and are awaiting the resurrection. If Hades is intended to be the temporary dwelling of departed metaphysical souls, then even the dead in the sea would be in that condition in that Hades. They are not. There is the one group who are those dead in the sea, and the other group is those who

---

[158] *Ewald M. Plass, Compiler. What Luther Says. (St. Louis, Concordia Publishing House, 1959), 625.*

are the dead in the grave, who are in Hades, their entombed condition in the ground.
3. In verse 14 we notice that "death and Hades were thrown into the lake of fire." If Hades represents "hell" then why is "hell," the place of hellfire, to be thrown into the lake of fire? This would seem to be rather redundant. But of course, the Scriptural intent here is again that Hades simply means the grave. Metaphorically death and the grave have come to outlive their usefulness and in effect are cast into the lake of fire, which represents utter destruction. After this judgment no physical human beings remain. All have either been changed to eternal immortal spiritual existence or have been cast into the lake of fire if they are the incorrigibly wicked. No longer will death take place and subsequently there is no further need for the grave. They are both done-away within God's annihilating lake of fire.
4. In verse 14 we also must notice that this casting into the lake of fire "is the second death," not immortal life in ever excruciating physical pain in the fires of a never-ending torturous flame. Death is the final end of the wicked, not eternal torture.

We see this concept in the Old Testament book of Malachi.

> Malachi 4:1 – 3 "For behold, the day is coming, burning like a furnace; and all the arrogant and every evildoer will be chaff; and the day that is coming will set them ablaze," says the Lord of hosts, "so that it will leave them neither root nor branch. But for you who fear My name, the sun of righteousness will rise with healing in its wings; and you will go forth and skip about like calves from the stall. You will tread down the wicked, for they will be ashes under the soles of your feet on the day which I am preparing." Says the Lord of hosts.

Being turned to ashes sounds a lot like the utter destruction of an annihilating fire to me. Coupled with other Scriptures which speak of the total destruction and death meted out to the wicked, there is no doubt that the wicked come to a state of nothingness and total non-existence in death. Psalm 73:27 is representative of many other such references.

> For those who are far from You will perish; You have destroyed all those who are unfaithful to You.

Neither the wicked nor do the righteous have immortal souls at this current contemporary point in the history of mankind. Only the righteous will become immortal at the second coming and others only later at the general resurrection and white throne judgment if they then accept salvation in Jesus Christ.

Malachi 4 totally eliminates and makes biblically impossible the doctrine of Universalism, since by the Lord's own words there will surely be those who are the "arrogant and every evildoer will be chaff, and the day that is coming will set them ablaze." This is why this writer cannot in good conscience accept pure Universalism.

The position of John Stott is good to consider in this matter. He writes of a number of Scripture texts which seem to indicate Universalism but he is also unconvinced that there will actually be none who will face hell. There are too many biblical references which speak of the ultimate destruction of the wicked in the lake of fire or Gehenna.

> These texts do not lead me to universalism, because of the many others which speak of the terrible and eternal reality of hell. But they do lead me to ask how God can in any meaningful sense be called 'everything to everybody' while an unspecified number of people still continue in rebellion against him and under his judgment. It would be easier to hold together the awful reality of hell and the universal reign of God if hell means destruction and the impenitent are no more.[159]

The truth of salvation lies somewhere in between massive annihilation of human beings occurring in the lake of fire, even of those who never heard, and Universalism. Essentially this writer sees the vast majority of mankind ultimately coming to salvation, but that salvation is subjectively conditional upon their acceptance of Jesus as Savior, either in this life or if they have been inadequately reached, then in the resurrection and judgment to come. In spite of the full opportunity people will receive in the kingdom age, Scripture demonstrates there still will be those who deny him and that they will be annihilated in the lake of fire.

TRADITIONAL ORTHODOX POSITION

John Walvoord, a major proponent of the traditional view of hell, sees in the annihilationism of Conditional Immortality a softening of the traditional stand on eternal punishment.

> Fourth, the view of hell as a *conditional* or temporary situation for the wicked has been advocated by many who find a contradiction between the doctrines of everlasting punishment and of a God of love and grace. As a result, they explain that hell is either temporary, in the sense that immortality is conditional and only

---

[159] David L. Edwards and John Stott. *Evangelical Essentials, A Liberal-Evangelical Dialogue.* (Downers Grove, InterVarsity Press, 1988), 319.

the righteous will be raised, or that it is redemptive, in the sense that whatever suffering there may be after this life because of sin will end up in the wicked being redeemed and restored to a place of blessing. In other words, conditional immortality or annihilation lessens the severity and the extent of everlasting punishment, while in universalism, all are eventually saved.[160]

Walvoord goes on to state his position regarding the traditional view of hell. He sees that the wicked suffer in hades in flaming fire during the intermediate state until the resurrection and then they are moved from hades to the lake of fire, to him, a place of eternal torment.

> The lake of fire does not provide annihilation but continual suffering. In Revelation 20:10, when the devil is cast into the lake of fire at the end of the millennium, the beast, the world ruler, and the false prophet who were thrown into the lake of fire at the beginning of the thousand-year reign of Christ are still there, sharing torment in the lake of fire with the devil "day and night for ever and ever." In Revelation 21:7 – 8 the unsaved are pictured as having their place "in the fiery lake of burning sulfur." Though the word *gehenna* is not used, the lake of fire is, and it serves as a synonym for the eternal place of torment.[161]

Gregory Beale also promotes the traditional view of hell and he sees "the second death" as eternal life. He envisions that the "second death" is actually eternal life in excruciating pain and suffering in the judgment of the lake of fire. Beale explains that the human soul endures spiritual suffering as an immortal being.

> The "lake of fire" has already been defined as unending, conscious punishment for all consigned to it. Now it is also termed "the second death." This is not a second physical death. The unbelievers undergoing judgment have already died physically and been resurrected. Revelation 20:10 shows that suffering the torment of the "lake of fire" does not involve physical death but suffering that is primarily spiritual in nature, since Satan and his angels are only spiritual beings. Corporeal suffering may be included for unbelieving humans, but only because they suffer spiritually while possessing resurrected bodies that never die physically.[162]

This quotation beautifully states the position of traditional Christianity

---

[160] John F. Walvoord, *Four Views On Hell*. William Crockett, General Editor. (Grand Rapids, Zondervan Publishing, 1996), 13.
[161] Ibid. 23.
[162] Gregory K. Beale, *Hell Under Fire*. General Editors, Christopher W. Morgan and Robert A. Peterson. (Grand Rapids, Zondervan Publishing, 2004), 130 – 131.

on hell. It also elegantly states the position of those who do not accept the mortality of the soul. For this traditional theological doctrine to hold it must be assumed that the soul is immortal and that it is a separate and metaphysical substance distinguished from the bodily life indicated in Genesis 2:7.

Scripture presents, contrary to popular traditional theology, that the soul is mortal, as has already been covered in depth, and that the resurrection of the unconverted will be a restoration to physical life for judgment. Only the saved are raised to immortal life in the first resurrection at the *parousia*. Jesus states that hell is a place where God destroys both bodies and souls. For God is able to "destroy both body and soul in hell (Matthew 10:28)." If the soul is destroyed in hell, how can it live on in immortality? Beale's statement that "the second death" means eternal spiritual life somehow does not seem to compute when compared to Jesus' statements in Scripture.

Beale likes to focus on Revelation 20:10 as a proof text for his position of eternal suffering. However, we need to remember the words of Jesus about this scenario.

> Matthew 25:41 Then He will also say to those on His left, 'Depart from Me, accursed ones, into the eternal fire which has been prepared for the devil and his angels;'

The primary reason for this eternal fire is for the punishment of "the devil and his angels." We must remember that the demonic beings have eternal life as they are spirit. It is they who will suffer eternally, but not human beings. Also physical fire cannot affect spirit. In a greater sense the fire that is prepared for the devil and his angels has more to do with some kind of eternal incarceration and separation from God for all eternity (Jude 6).

It is very likely that the beast and false prophet of Revelation 20:10 are in fact the demons who inhabited and guided the human figures they directed. They constitute two persons of the unholy trinity of Revelation 16:13 – 14.

> And I saw coming out of the mouth of the dragon and out of the mouth of the beast and out of the mouth of the false prophet, three unclean spirits like frogs; for they are spirits of demons, performing signs, which go out to the kings of the whole world, to gather them together for the war of the great day of God, the Almighty.

In this passage, John may be revealing the spiritual side of the story while Daniel offers the fate of the physical human beast. In Daniel 7:11 we read of the outcome of the judgment of the beast.

> Then I kept looking because of the sound of the boastful words

> which the horn was speaking; I kept looking until the beast was slain, and its body was destroyed and given to the burning fire.

Daniel definitely describes the physical death of the individual known as the Beast, who has a body which "was destroyed and given to the burning fire." Daniel pictures the annihilation of the human being known as the Beast. John's Revelation may reveal the destiny of the demonic spirit which possessed the Beast.

One may also consider that if Revelation 20:10 actually means that human beings will live in the terrible agony of the lake of fire forever in excruciating pain and suffering, how can that be compatible with the statement we see only a few verses later in Revelation 21:3 – 4? If God will wipe away all the tears of the eyes of his people and if death and mourning and crying and pain have all passed away, how then does that square with the traditional Christian doctrine of eternal pain and suffering, mourning and crying of tears in hell?

The traditional concept of everlasting hellfire does not square with Scripture. Scripture reveals that souls are mortal, they can and do die, that the wicked are burned to ashes and absolutely destroyed and annihilated. Since they no longer exist they will not cry or mourn or have pain or again suffer death. They will be dead and non-existent for eternity. That is eternal punishment, not eternal punishing.

UNQUENCHABLE FIRE

There seems to be confusion regarding biblical usage of the term "unquenchable fire." In Mark 9:43 Jesus warns about going to "unquenchable fire."

> If your hand causes you to stumble, cut it off; it is better for you to enter life crippled, than, having your two hands, to go into hell, into the unquenchable fire.

The Greek word translated "unquenchable" is *asbestos*. *Asbestos* translates as follows according to Danker and Bauer:

> *Asbestos*: of something whose state of being cannot be nullified or stopped; hence 1. of fire *inextinguishable*.[163]

When it comes to exegesis of this word in Scripture expositors tend to use it in the sense of being eternally inextinguishable. Subsequently it

---

[163] *Frederick William Danker, Editor. Walter Bauer's A Greek-English Lexicon of the New Testament and other Early Christian literature, Third edition. (Chicago, University of Chicago Press, 2000), 141.*

receives the sense of being the eternally existent punishing hell fire of traditional theology to which the wicked are subject for all the unending future.

We see in ancient literature that this is not the intended understanding. The first century Jewish historian Josephus speaks of the wood for the sacrificial altar in the temple of Jerusalem and that the flames of the altar were *asbestos,* "unquenchable."

> Now the next day was the festival of Xylophory; upon which the custom was for every one to bring wood for the altar, (that there might never be a want of fuel for that fire which was unquenchable and always burning.)[164]

There is only one major translation problem here for biblical scholars. This *asbestos*, unquenchable fire on the sacrificial altar, was quenched by the Romans in 70 AD. This unquenchable fire had also been quenched previously by Nebuchadnezzar and the Babylonians in 585 BC. How can an unquenchable fire be quenched? Obviously our interpretation of the term leaves something to be desired. Obviously the endurance of the fire cannot be taken to be for eternity. Rather, by actual usage, the flame is unquenchable while it is performing its work. Thereafter it can be extinguished. It is quite apparent that this is the intended meaning of the "unquenchable fire" as applied to the judgment in Scripture. While it is accomplishing its work of annihilating the wicked it is unquenchable. When its work is finished, and the wicked are rendered completely lifeless and no longer existent, when they have been turned to ashes (Malachi 4:3), then and only then will God himself extinguish the flames.

> God's victory ushers in the judgment of the living and the dead. The righteous will inherit eternal life. The evil, eternal judgment, or alternatively, eternal nonbeing.[165]

GOD, THE UNQUENCHABLE FIRE

Let us recall the original source of this unquenchable flame. The source of the flame on the sacrificial altar at the tabernacle in the wilderness was God himself.

> Leviticus 9:23 – 24 Moses and Aaron went into the tent of meeting. When they came out and blessed the people, the glory of the Lord appeared to all the people. Then fire came out from before the Lord and consumed the burnt offering and the portions

---

[164] *William Whiston, A.M., translator. Josephus Complete Works. (Grand Rapids, Kregel Publications, 1969), 491.*
[165] *Walter Wink, The Human Being. (Minneapolis, Fortress Press, 2002), 159.*

of fat on the altar; and when all the people saw it, they shouted and fell on their faces.

At the inauguration of Solomon's temple the very same manifestation occurred. Immediately after Solomon's dedicatory prayer God answered with his approval by the fire that was to serve the temple sacrificial system.

> 2 Chronicles 7:1 – 3 Now when Solomon had finished praying, fire came down from heaven and consumed the burnt offering and the sacrifices, and the glory of the Lord filled the house. The priests could not enter into the house of the Lord because the glory of the Lord filled the Lord's house. All the sons of Israel, seeing the fire come down and the glory of the Lord upon the house, bowed down on the pavement with their faces to the ground, and they worshiped and gave praise to the Lord, saying, "Truly He is good, truly His lovingkindness is everlasting."

This unquenchable flame was to be kept burning as a sacred responsibility of the priests. They were not to allow it to be extinguished.

> Leviticus 6:9 & 12 – 13 Command Aaron and his sons, saying, 'This is the law for the burnt offering; the burnt offering itself shall remain on the hearth on the altar all night until the morning, and the fire on the altar is to be kept burning on it....The fire on the altar shall be kept burning on it. It shall not go out, but the priest shall burn wood on it every morning; and he shall layout the burnt offering on it, and offer up in smoke the fat portions of the peace offerings on it. Fire shall be kept burning continually on the altar; it is not to go out.

Regarding the unquenchable fires of hell, there can be a limited time duration for their existence according to Scripture. We err if we assign a definition of eternal duration to the fires of judgment. Scripture is clear that when God sends forth his fire of wrath, no one has the power to extinguish it but himself.

> Jeremiah 4:4 Circumcise yourselves to the Lord and remove the foreskins of your heart, men of Judah and inhabitants of Jerusalem, or else My wrath will go forth like fire and burn with none to quench it, because of the evil of your deeds.

Willem A. VanGemeren writes of the powerful impact that the message of the prophets had whenever they referred to God's fiery power. God's fiery presence drove away all opposition to him.

> Further, they shattered human ideologies, structures, and popular misconceptions by challenging people to discern whether this

God will come *for* or *against* them. The prophets asked rhetorically, "Who can withstand his indignation? Who can endure his fierce anger?" The prophets sounded a discordant note whenever they spoke of God's being a consuming fire. For example, Micah said:

> 'Look! The Lord is coming from his dwelling place; he comes down and treads the high places of the earth. The mountains melt beneath him and the valleys split apart, like wax before the fire, like water rushing down a slope. All this is because of Jacob's transgression.' (Micah 1:3 – 5)[166]

Odom comments on Jude 7 and characterizes the statement that the cities of Sodom and Gomorrah, as having suffered "the vengeance of eternal fire," as a statement of the power of God. In his view the people are not suffering eternally but rather that they were consumed in the flames of a fire which is in effect eternal since it is used to describe the nature of God himself. *For our God is a consuming fire* (Hebrews 12:29).

> Note particularly that those wicked cities are "set forth as an example, suffering the vengeance of eternal fire." It is not the suffering that is said to be eternal, but the fire that God employed to destroy them is eternal in its effect.
>
> Some suppose that the words "unquenchable fire" mean that there is an eternally burning hell in which the wicked will writhe in torment and anguish ages without end. Such is not the intention of John in saying: "He [Christ] will burn up the chaff with unquenchable fire." Matthew 3:12; Luke 3:17. By the word "unquenchable" he means fire that no man can extinguish or put out. Chaff is very easily consumed by fire, and John very plainly says that Christ will "burn up" – utterly consume – those (the chaff) it figuratively represents.[167]

Unquenchable fire is therefore used to denote the irresistibility of God's judgment which is used to utterly consume the wicked. Edward Fudge characterizes John the Baptist as understanding the irresistible consumption of God when he spoke of the coming One who would baptize with fire.

> The Son of Man would suffer, the Lamb would die in silence, but John predicts that this same one would come again as Judge. 'His winnowing fork is in his hand, and he will clear his threshing floor, gathering the wheat into his barn and burning up the chaff with the unquenchable fire (Matt. 3:12). As in the Old Testament, 'unquenchable fire' represents a fire of judgment which cannot

---

[166] Willem A. VanGemeren, *Interpreting The Prophetic Word.* (Grand Rapids, Zondervan Publishing House, 1990), 219.
[167] Robert Leo Odom, *Is Your Soul Immortal?* (Ukiah, CA., Orion Publishing, 2007), 70.

be stopped. On and on it comes, driven by the wind of God's righteous fury – burning irresistibly, until nothing is left but silence and smoke. The Old Testament scriptures give ample background for understanding his judgment-fire; like them, John sees it as 'burning up' the chaff.[168]

FUDGE'S VIEW

In opposition to Gregory K. Beale, we have the testimony of a man who is considered to be the foremost authority on Conditionalism in contemporary Christianity. Edward William Fudge states with true elegance and biblical rationality his thoughts regarding the final punishment of the wicked.

> The fact is that the Bible does not teach the traditional view of final punishment. Scripture nowhere suggests that God is an eternal torturer. It never says the damned will writhe in ceaseless torment or that the glories of heaven will forever be blighted by the screams from hell. The idea of conscious everlasting torment was a grievous mistake, a horrible error, a gross slander against the heavenly Father, whose character we truly see in the life of Jesus of Nazareth.
>
> Scripture teaches instead that those who go to hell will experience "everlasting destruction" in "the second death," for God is able to "destroy both body and soul in hell." The actual process of destruction may well involve conscious pain that differs in magnitude in each individual case – Scripture seems to indicate that it will. Whatever the case, God's judgment will be measured by perfect, holy, divine justice. Even hell will demonstrate the absolute righteousness of God. From Genesis to Revelation, the Bible repeatedly warns that the wicked will "die," "perish" or "be destroyed." Those who die this second death will never live again [169]

Robert W. Yarbrough challenges the above quotation of Fudge. He questions Fudge's statement in opposition to the perspective that "the glories of heaven will forever be blighted by the screams from hell."

> Similarly, "the glories of heaven" will not "forever be blighted by the screams from hell." Scripture implies that the smoke from the judgment of God's enemies will not mar heavenly praise but if anything enhance it (Rev. 14:11; 19:3). Furthermore, in heaven

---

[168] *Edward William Fudge, The Fire That Consumes. (Milton Keynes, Paternoster Digital Library, 2005), 95.*
[169] *Edward William Fudge and Robert A. Peterson, Two Views Of Hell, A Biblical and Theological Dialogue. (Downers Grove, Intervarsity Press, 2000), 20 – 21.*

"there will be no more death or mourning or crying or pain, for the old order of things has passed away" (21:4). So hell's woes will ultimately be transcended by those blessed in the heavenly presence. This may appear callous at first glance, but it is what Scripture says, and as Fudge agrees, this is the main issue in the debate.[170]

There seems to be inadequate understanding on Yarbrough's part regarding the Scriptures that he is quoting and commenting upon. First, Revelation 14:11 speaks only of the doom of the worshippers of the beast and says absolutely nothing about its enhancement of heavenly worship.

That whole idea that somehow the suffering of those in hell enhances the worship and praise of God is a sadistically monstrous teaching that has no authentic origin in Scripture. Clark Pinnock makes the point well as to how the saved do not delight in the pains of the damned, and that we must mature spiritually and jettison this "dismal set of ideas" as heresy, in order that the genuine gospel may begin to regain some respect.

> In closing, I propose turning the tables on the whole issue of hell in the tradition. Rather than insisting that the view of hell is everlasting conscious torment remain a defining characteristic of orthodox doctrine, we should be throwing it over. In fact, the entire set of beliefs surrounding hell, including unending torture, double predestination, and the delight that the saints are supposed to feel at the pains of the damned, does orthodox theology absolutely no good. This set of dismal ideas should be dumped in the name of credible doctrine. Why should sound doctrine have such burdens to bear: If we would clean up our act, it might even be possible to save hell as an intelligible belief.[171]

Second, Revelation 19:3 speaks of the destruction of the city of Babylon the great and the fact that it is "burned up with fire" (18:8). Revelation 19:3 is a celebration of that destruction as we notice that the smoke rises "forever and ever", or in the Greek, for an *aion* or an age or era, a human lifetime,[172] a specific period of time. This does not necessarily mean for eternity as we envision the use of the word. There is no mention of the fire burning forever, nor is there mention of their being in a state of pain and suffering forever, for the city has been "burned up." This would rather indicate complete desolation and annihilation.

---

[170] *Robert W. Yarbrough, Hell Under Fire, Chapter 3. General Editors, Christopher W. Morgan and Robert A. Peterson. (Grand Rapids, Zondervan Publishing, 2004), 78.*
[171] *Clark H. Pinnock, William Crockett, General Editor. Four Views On Hell. (Grand Rapids, Zondervan, 1996), 162-163.*
[172] *Joseph H. Thayer, Thayer's Greek-English Lexicon Of The New Testament. (Grand Rapids, Baker Book House, 1984), 18 – 19.*

Yarborough refers to Revelation 21:4 and its focus on the absolute cessation of death, mourning, crying and pain but sees that condition as existing in heaven. Revelation does not place this condition in heaven but rather upon earth (Vss. 1 – 2). Even the New Jerusalem is not to be relegated to heaven. It too comes to earth (Vs. 10). In the greater scheme of things in Scripture, heaven comes to earth rather than the inhabitants of earth going to heaven.

> Likewise, the pictures of heaven in the book of Revelation have been much misunderstood. The wonderful description in Revelation 4 and 5 of the twenty-four elders casting their crowns before the throne of God and the lamb, beside the sea of glass, is not, despite one of Charles Wesley's great hymns, a picture of the last day, with all the redeemed in heaven at last. It is a picture of present reality, the heavenly dimension of our present life. Heaven, in the Bible, is not a future destiny but the other, hidden, dimension of our ordinary life – God's dimension, if you like. God made heaven and earth; at the last he will remake both and join them together forever. And when we come to the picture of the actual end in Revelation 21 – 22, we find not ransomed souls making their way to a disembodied heaven but rather the new Jerusalem coming down from heaven to earth, uniting the two in a lasting embrace.[173]

LUTHER

Martin Luther's view of hell did not accept the immediacy of such miserable existence nor punishment upon death. Most likely his Thnetopsychist view, that the soul is mortal and that it is metaphorically asleep in the grave, also governed his perspective on hell. Since the soul is not immortal, therefore the soul is not alive in the intermediate state. Therefore there is no need for hell until the time of the general judgment since no one is alive in the intermediate state so as to be in existence in either heaven or hell at this current moment. In a sermon he gave on October 28, 1535, Luther defined his thoughts regarding the place and time of the implementation of the punishments of hell.

> I am as yet not too sure what hell really is like before the Last Day. For I think nothing of the picture of the artists and the preaching of belly servers according to which it is supposed to be a particular place in which the damned souls now exist. After all, the devils themselves are not yet in hell but, Peter says (2 Peter 2:4), are reserved for hell in bonds; and St. Paul calls them the rulers

---

[173] *N.T. Wright, Surprised By Hope. (New York, Harper Collins, 2008), 18-19.*

and the mighty ones of this world who move about in the upper air (Eph. 6:12). Moreover, Christ calls the devil the prince of this world (John 12:31). But this could certainly not be true if the devils were in hell….to be sure, however, matters will take a different turn on the Last Day. Then hell will be a particular place, where those will be who are condemned to hell or to the eternal wrath of God. But enough of this. It is of little importance whether a person holds hell to be what men now paint or picture it to be. No doubt it now is, and will be, far worse than anyone is able to describe, picture, or think it to be.[174]

To Luther neither the place of hell-fire nor its implementation as a punishment for unbelievers was a consideration for any concern at the moment. Eternal punishment would not be a reality until the time of the judgment on the Last Day. This timing and condition then serves well the notion of the resurrection of the saints on the day of Jesus' second coming and the later resurrection of unbelievers before the Great White Throne Judgment. How redundant and unnecessary would a resurrection from the grave of believers be if they were already actually in blissful existence in heaven? How sadistic and unmerciful to bring up hordes of unbelievers, from an eternal hell-fire of excruciating pain and suffering, just to announce to them that they will now be judged for their sins only to have sentence pronounced upon them and to be recast into hell with absolutely no opportunity for repentance and confession. Luther saw no such condition for either believers or unbelievers. Luther's position was that the soul is mortal, it dies at the dissolution of the body from the breath of God and is in a state of complete non-existence during the intermediate state with no need of heavenly nor hellish existence for anyone since all are truly dead and non existent in the interim. Luther was a Conditionalist.

The Corinthian Church of Paul's day was primarily a Gentile Greek church. Because of their previous platonic philosophical beliefs, the Corinthians carried the baggage of pagan perspectives into the Christian Church. One of these beliefs regarded the soul and the afterlife. In Greek philosophy the soul was partnered with the body until the death of the body and then the soul was set free from the shackles of the physical host. There was no thought in platonic philosophy of the future resurrection of the imprisoning and corrupting evil physical body. Such a hope was incomprehensible to the Greek mindset, which saw only the immortal and immaterial soul as having any value or worth. Consequently, the Apostle Paul had his hands full in reeducating the Corinthian Church regarding the

---

[174] *Ewald M. Plass, Compiler. What Luther Says. (Saint Louis, Concordia Publishing House, 1959), 625 – 626*

body, spirit, and subsequent soul life of a human being. Frank Thielman comments on Paul's attempt to reeducate the Corinthians in his corrective letter to them.

> A second aspect of Paul's argument focuses on the future consequences of the Corinthians' insistence that believers will not be raised from the dead. Paul refuses to allow what the Corinthians seem to assume – that the immortality of the disembodied soul can be substituted for the notion of a bodily resurrection. Without a bodily resurrection, Paul insists there will be no immortality at all (15:18 – 19). Death will not be defeated (15:26, 54 – 55), and this life will be the sum total of Christian existence (15:19). The inscription commonly used on Roman graves will be right: *non fui, fui, non sum, non curo* – "I was not, I was, I am not, I care not."[175]

Paul emphasizes the Christian view with the Corinthians as he focuses on the coming resurrection to immortality, which will be brought to fruition at the return of Christ. Though the body has dissolved in the grave and the spirit God gave at conception returned to him who gave it, yet, these elements will be reunited, made anew and imperishable. Our newly imparted immortal life, or soul, will be manifest in its created glory in believers only, at the second coming.

> I Corinthians 15:50 – 58 Now I say this, brethren, that flesh and blood cannot inherit the kingdom of God; nor does the perishable inherit the imperishable. Behold, I tell you a mystery; we will not all sleep, but we will all be changed, in a moment, in the twinkling of an eye, at the last trumpet; for the trumpet will sound, and the dead will be raised imperishable, and we will be changed. For this perishable must put on the imperishable, and this mortal must put on immortality. But when this perishable will have put on the imperishable, and this mortal will have put on immortality, then will come about the saying that is written, "death is swallowed up in victory. O death where is your victory? O death where is your sting?" The sting of death is sin, and the power of sin is the law; but thanks be to God, who gives us the victory through our Lord Jesus Christ. Therefore, my beloved brethren, be steadfast, immovable, always abounding in the work of the Lord, knowing that your toil is not in vain in the Lord.

In this, Paul is reflecting the thoughts of the Lord on the matter. Jesus looked forward to the resurrection, but not only that, he also reveals to us in

---

[175] *Frank Thielman, Theology of the New Testament. (Grand Rapids, Zondervan, 2005), 304.*

his quotation from Isaiah 54:13 that the day will come, future tense, when "they shall all be taught of God."

> John 6:44 – 45 No one can come to Me unless the Father who sent Me draws him; and I will raise him up on the last day. It is written in the prophets 'and they shall all be taught of God.' Everyone who has heard and learned from the Father, comes to Me.

> Isaiah 54:13 All your sons will be taught of the Lord; and the well-being of your sons will be great.

Robert Leo Odom recognizes that the biblical "second death" is final. If one suffers the second death there is no further hope of evangelism for that person nor of a return to life.

> With Him 'is the fountain of life" (Psalm 36:9), and by rejecting Him as the Source of life, the unrepentant sinner dooms himself to perish – to die "the second death." There will be no second chance after that. From the second death there will be no resurrection. Impenitent sinners will suffer eternal annihilation.[176]

Unfortunately the Conditionalist view is not the majority opinion in Christianity today. However, one may take some comfort in sharing this view with some rather influential and trustworthy theologically sound persons such as Wycliffe, Luther, Tyndale, and Origen. Origen is known as "the first repudiator of an eternal hell."[177] In fact as a result of his teachings against the unending tortures of hell, though he was probably the most prolific writer and influential theologian of the early church, the Emperor Justinian condemned Origen as a heretic in the 6th century, about three hundred years after his death.

After this study, it is easy to agree with Fudge when he says: "Those who die this second death will never live again."[178] The Bible does not support the immortality of the soul, nor does it support everlasting conscious torment in a never-ending hell fire. On the other hand the Bible does support the final consumption and destruction of those who refuse salvation in Christ. That destruction and consumption is final and they will never live again. This too reflects the mercy and grace of God since everlasting life for them would truly be "hell" if they were to be forever under the authority of the Lord.

---

[176] Robert Leo Odom, *Is Your Soul Immortal? (Ukiah, CA., Orion Publishing, 2007), 74 – 75.*
[177] Hans Urs Von Balthasar, *Dare We Hope "That All Men Be Saved"? (San Francisco, Ignatius Press, 1988), 59.*
[178] Edward William Fudge and Robert A. Peterson, *Two Views Of Hell, A Biblical and Theological Dialogue. (Downers Grove, Intervarsity Press, 2000), 21.*

> Psalm 104:35 Let sinners be consumed from the earth and let the wicked be no more. Bless the Lord, O my soul. Praise the Lord!

In summary, chapter seven reveals the fallacy of traditional thinking regarding eternal hell fire. The lake of fire is composed of God himself and his vengeance upon the unyielding wicked will be unquenchable while it is accomplishing its purpose of annihilation of the wicked. The lake of fire will then cease its work upon their consumption to death and their liquidation into ashes. At that point they no longer are a soul that exists. Edward William Fudge, the foremost authority on Conditionalism in contemporary Christianity, sees clearly the total obliteration of the wicked in the lake of fire. From the viewpoint of the Reformation, Martin Luther also held the same position that the wicked will face the judgment of God but that it would not take place until the eschaton. To Luther, no one today is suffering in the flames of hell.

This material now opens the door to discussion of whether or not God would deal mercifully and graciously with those who have opposed him. Chapter Eight will focus on God's grace and the scriptural fact that he will not punish anyone who has been truly ignorant of him and his offer of salvation.

CHAPTER EIGHT
GOD'S GRACE

CHAPTER EIGHT

GOD'S GRACE

*God holds people accountable for what they have been given,
Not for what they have failed to hear.*[179]

This work began with a focus on man's ignorance in chapter one. It is now finally time to redirect the focus to God's Grace. The Scriptures reveal a God of true justice tempered with profuse mercy.

GOD DOES NOT PUNISH FOR IGNORANCE

In the scriptural evidence mentioned thus far, especially in Chapter Two, we have seen the biblical truth establishing the fact that God will not punish us for our ignorance. As has been demonstrated by many of the sources that have been cited, there are those who agree with this position. One additional writer, Greg Albrecht, also sees that God is so loving of his children that he withholds judgment on sins that we have committed in ignorance. In an article related to this topic, he answers a reader's question as to whether God would send people to hell because of their ignorance in following the teaching of a false prophet.

> I most emphatically do not agree that God sends anyone to hell because they, for some reason best known to God, were deceived and mesmerized by a spiritual Pied Piper. Such a conclusion would contradict the biblical definition of God as love. Will God punish false prophets? Again, if followers of a false prophet can be sincerely deceived, so too can a false prophet. Having said that, I also believe, because there are ample biblical references to this reality, there are false prophets who know better. In that case, God will judge them—but again, I absolutely resist the idea of an eternal torment in hell. I see many biblical objections to eternal torment in hell—and, on the other hand, much that is religious tradition.[180]

Albrecht understands that much of Christian traditional teaching is at fault regarding the crisis of misunderstanding the Scriptures that we have in the Christian canon today. No loving Father would ever assign his child to

---

[179] John Sanders, *What About Those Who Have Never Heard?* (Downers Grove, Intervarsity Press, 1995), 143.
[180] Greg Albrecht, *Does God Send People To Hell Because Of Their Ignorance?* Plain Truth Ministries, October 25, 2010 PTM Update.www.ptm.org/uni/resources/ptmupdate/102510/1.html.

excruciating and endless torture for all eternity. The very thought is monstrous. No, rather God loves his children and would never allow such a harsh penalty for a momentary few years of neglect and rejection. The Bible teaches that the rebellious sons of God will suffer indeed, but not for an eternity. The wicked will be burned until they are consumed and in that consumption will cease to exist. They will suffer excruciating pain, yes, but for only a relatively short period of time, of God's determination, and then their bodies will become ashes in his consumptive flames.

We have previously cited Malachi 4:3 as a biblical demonstration of this fact of consumptive annihilation. There are also other Scriptures which support this end. In 2 Samuel 23:6 – 7, King David speaks of the worthless wicked in his last song before his death.

> But the worthless, everyone of them will be thrust away like thorns, because they cannot be taken in hand; but the man who touches them must be armed with iron and the shaft of a spear, and they will be completely burned with fire in their place.

Ezekiel speaks of the King of Tyre as a type of Satan, and illustrates the end of the wicked in what will happen to him. He is both burned to ashes and he ceases to be forever.

> Ezekiel 28:18 – 19 By the multitude of your iniquities, in the unrighteousness of your trade you profaned your sanctuaries. Therefore I have brought fire from the midst of you; it has consumed you, and I have turned you to ashes on the earth in the eyes of all who see you. All who know you among the peoples are appalled at you; you have become terrified and you will cease to be forever.

The New Testament also gives us clear instruction regarding the judgment. If one receives the knowledge of the truth and still rejects it, then the fiery judgment of God will indeed fall on those individuals. But please notice that judgment will not take place until after they have received the truth though they are still in rebellion against it.

> Hebrews 10:26 – 27 For if we go on sinning willfully after receiving the knowledge of the truth, there no longer remains a sacrifice for sins, but a terrifying expectation of judgment and the fury of a fire which will consume the adversaries.

The Apostle Peter speaks of Sodom and Gomorrah having been reduced to ashes as an example of what would happen to those who would continue in rebellion. That rebellion and ungodly living would result in their becoming ashes as well.

> 2 Peter 2:6 and if He condemned the cities of Sodom and Gomorrah to destruction by reducing them to ashes, having made them an example to those who would live ungodly lives thereafter;

These verses all exhibit the biblical fact that the wicked will be consumed and reduced to ashes by the consumptive fire of God. None of these passages indicate ongoing eternal suffering or agony. The agony is temporary for whatever period of time God allots for the punishment of those who hate him. Their end is eternal death, not eternal life in hell. Their end is to be turned to ashes rather than continuing in bodily and conscious suffering in blistering pain and misery for eternity. Their end is eternal death, not an immortal eternal life of conscious misery.

In all of this, God is merciful and gracious even to those who hate him. In the end those few children who will finally reject him will be put out of their misery, and ours, through their extinction.

GOD'S GRACE MUST BE TAUGHT

The grace of God has been exhibited toward us since an antiquity that we are simply incapable of understanding. In his incomprehensible intelligence, God knew us, chose us, and predestined us to be his sons and his chosen people long before he created this world.

> Ephesians 1:4 – 8 just as He chose us in Him before the foundation of the world, that we would be holy and blameless before Him. In love He predestined us to adoption as sons through Jesus Christ to Himself, according to the kind intention of His will, to the praise of the glory of His grace, which He freely bestowed on us in the Beloved. In Him we have redemption through His blood, the forgiveness of our trespasses, according to the riches of His grace which He lavished on us. In all wisdom and insight.

Contrary to Calvin, it is apparent that the Lord is showing us in this passage that all humanity has been predestined to be adopted as sons through Jesus Christ to himself. Jesus accomplished all that is required for our salvation by his perfect offering of his blood on Calvary. Objectively our salvation has been accomplished in Christ. Subjectively however, we must consciously accept the salvation he has bestowed on us in order to complete the salvation covenant. He did the work of salvation in our stead and we must accept it in a cognizant state of understanding.

This principle is illustrated in the conversion of the jailer and his household in Acts 16. When the jailer asked "What must I do to be saved?" in verse 30, Paul and Silas answered and instructed him with the result being the baptism of his whole household.

> Acts 16:31 – 33 They said, "Believe in the Lord Jesus, and you will be saved, you and your household." And they spoke the word of the Lord to him together with all who were in his house. And he took them that very hour of the night and washed their wounds, and immediately he was baptized, he and all his household.

Speaking and teaching them the word of God, was both convicting and necessary for their understanding of what they were accepting. It is the word of God, not the vain philosophies of men, that brings us to salvation.

I cringe at the words of some, who balk at teaching our people the word of God in all its unvarnished truth. They would rather play games, institute programs, develop supposedly clever alternatives to "dull, dry, boring lecturers" which focus on biblical teaching. Our churches are suffering as people are being starved for the genuine gospel of Scripture and our congregations are showing the symptoms of the lack of biblical focus as they become more spiritually immature, emotionally disturbed, and susceptible to strange, false and cultic teachings. Keeping our focus on the word of God keeps us both spiritually safe and sane. Today's church could use much more of it.

Some believe that our young people do not appreciate a "too cerebral" approach to the biblical education we are giving. That attitude does not give our young people enough credit and respect regarding their learning capabilities and desire to know the Lord. One has to ask, do we wish to mimic public education standards which have been "dumbing down" our educational expectations for years? In the same manner do we also disrespect the ability of our congregants to comprehend the deeper matters of the gospel and likewise end up "dumbing down" the church?

The gospel is "cerebral" by design and nature and must be well taught and properly understood before we can have an adequate knowledge of what God has done for us, what his plan is and what our response is expected to be. Without that comprehension we cannot have a deep appreciation of his salvation and its assorted blessings. Without adequate biblical education our members become spiritually immature and easily susceptible to deception. As pastors, in the priestly function of teaching the word of God to the people of God, we are responsible for the sacred calling of preserving, teaching and applying the word of God. If we neglect and fail in our responsibility, the Lord may ultimately see to it that we are disqualified and replaced by those who honor, respect and fear him with deepest respect in their sacred service.

> Hosea 4:6 My people are destroyed for lack of knowledge. Because you have rejected knowledge, I also will reject you from being My priest. Since you have forgotten the law of your God, I

also will forget your children.

It is time for spiritual renewal and revival among the pastorate. It is time for us to personally immerse ourselves in the powerfully efficacious word of God and willingly, lovingly and respectfully teach it to our congregations. They certainly can and will learn if only we will teach.

> 2 Timothy 3:16 – 17 All Scripture is inspired by God and profitable for teaching, for reproof, for correction, for training in righteousness; so that the man of God may be adequate, equipped for every good work.

We have no right to teach a watered down gospel. Pleasing the ears of men while denying the realities of the revealed word of Scripture will bring God's judgment. In his instructions to the young pastor Timothy, Paul instructed him with this admonition:

> 2 Timothy 4:1 – 4 I solemnly charge you in the presence of God and of Christ Jesus, who is to judge the living and the dead, and by His appearing and His kingdom: preach the word; be ready in season and out of season; reprove, rebuke, exhort, with great patience and instruction. For the time will come when they will not endure sound doctrine; but wanting to have their ears tickled, they will accumulate for themselves teachers in accordance to their own desires, and will turn away their ears from the truth and will turn aside to myths.

J.I. Packer notes how the Christian church of our day diminishes any focus on God's judgment and wrath. It is manifest in attempts to minimize the importance of repentance by defining it solely as "a turning to God." In its fuller definition, repentance includes "feeling remorse" for sin.[181]

> Second, to beget a true fear in our souls for God. "Let us have grace whereby we may serve God acceptably with reverence and godly fear: for our God is a consuming fire" (Heb. 12:28, 29). We cannot serve Him "acceptably" unless there is due "reverence" for His awful Majesty and "godly fear" of His righteous anger, and these are best promoted by frequently calling to mind that "our God is a consuming fire." Third, to draw out our soul in fervent praise [to Jesus Christ] for having delivered us from "the wrath to come" (I Thess. 1:10). Our readiness or our reluctancy to meditate upon the wrath of God becomes a sure test of how our hearts really stand affected towards Him.[182]

---

[181] *Walter Bauer, A Greek-English Lexicon Of The New Testament And Other Early Christian Literature, Third Edition. Frederick William Danker, Editor. (Chicago, University of Chicago Press, 2000), 640.*

[182] *J.I. Packer, Knowing God. (Downer's Grove, InterVarsity Press, 1993), 157.*

Walter Bauer's definition of "repentance" is demonstrated in my own denomination's *Statement of Beliefs.* We have a position on repentance which includes "an awareness of personal sinfulness."

> Repentance toward God is a change of mind and attitude in response to the grace of God prompted by the Holy Spirit and grounded in the Word of God. It includes awareness of personal sinfulness and trust in and allegiance to Jesus Christ through whom all humanity has been reconciled to God and accompanies a new life sanctified by the Holy Spirit through faith in Jesus Christ.[183]

In 2 Peter 3:9 we read that God is "not willing for any to perish but for all to come to repentance." If God wants all people to come to repentance, are we pastors preaching about the importance of repentance? If it is the Lord's desire that no one perishes, are we teaching a message of God's intent and desire to save all people?

Those who do not come to salvation are those who make the deliberate choice to reject the truth of salvation. Salvation is only for those who accept and love the truth. Loving the truth requires that one is actually taught the truth. Rather "cerebral" isn't it?

> 2 Thessalonians 2:8 – 13 Then that lawless one will be revealed whom the Lord will slay with the breath of His mouth and bring to an end by the appearance of His coming; that is, the one whose coming is in accord with the activity for Satan with all power and signs and false wonders, and with all the deception of wickedness for those who perish, because they did not receive the love of the truth so as to be saved. For this reason God will send upon them a deluding influence so that they will believe what is false, in order that they all may be judged who did not believe the truth, but took pleasure in wickedness. But we should always give thanks to God for you, brethren beloved by the Lord, because God has chosen you from the beginning for salvation through sanctification by the Spirit and faith in the truth.

CHARIS

We must consider the Greek word that is used to define grace if we are to have a firmer idea of what is meant by the grace of God in Scripture. The primary word used in the New Testament is the Greek charis and it is defined here from Strong's Enhanced Concordance.

---

[183] *Grace Communion International, Statement Of Beliefs, (Glendora, CA., 2009), 10.*

1. That which affords joy, pleasure, delight, sweetness, charm, loveliness. Grace of speech.
2. Good will, loving-kindness, favour. Of the merciful kindness by which God, exerting his holy influence upon souls, turns them to Christ, keeps, strengthens, increases them in Christian faith, knowledge, affection, and kindles them to the exercise of the Christian virtues.
3. What is due to grace. The spiritual condition of one governed by the power of divine grace. The token or proof of grace, benefit. A gift of grace. Benefit, bounty.
4. Thanks, (for benefits, services, favours), recompense, reward.[184]

In reading this definition, it is apparent that grace is something given by God without our merit. It is his gift, which is bestowed upon us out of his loving-kindness and is altogether undeserved on our part. In spite of the fact that *all have sinned and fall short of the glory of God* (Romans 3:23), in his love and merciful grace he still *desires all men to be saved and to come to the knowledge of the truth* (I Timothy 2:4).

It is only by the grace of God, through his unmerited favor, that we have any hope of salvation. By his grace we are called, by his grace we are granted the gift of repentance, by his grace we are granted the very faith of Jesus our Lord, by his grace we are saved, and by his grace we are granted the very indwelling of the Holy Spirit.

According to Scripture the Holy Spirit does not indwell all people. We are told in Romans that there are conditions which must be met before the Holy Spirit dwells in us.

> Romans 8:9 – 11 However, you are not in the flesh but in the Spirit, if indeed the Spirit of God dwells in you. But if anyone does not have the Spirit of Christ, he does not belong to Him. If Christ is in you, though the body is dead because of sin, yet the spirit is alive because of righteousness. But if the Spirit of Him who raised Jesus from the dead dwells in you, He who raised Christ Jesus from the dead will also give life to your mortal bodies through His Spirit who dwells in you.

There are a number of important factors which come forth from this passage. It is critical to understand that this book of Romans is addressed to believers, the saints in the city of Rome. It is not intended to designate the state of all humanity (Romans 1:4 – 8).

---

[184] *James Strong, The Exhaustive Concordance of the Bible: Showing every word of the Text of the Common English Version of the Canonical Books, and Every Occurrence of Each Word in Regular Order. Electronic edition. (Ontario, Woodside Bible Fellowship, 1996).*

First, in this passage we notice that these believers are not considered to be a part of the fleshly and carnally focused world around them. They rather have their eyes and lives fixed on the Spirit, but that spiritual perspective is granted them only because they have the Spirit of God dwelling in them. Not only that, but for those who do not have the Spirit of Christ, they do not belong to Christ. Consequently, only those who are indwelt by the Holy Spirit, the Third Person of the Trinity, they, and only they, are the children of God.

Second, we see that our sinful living and state of mind has brought us to a condition deserving of death. We are, on the other hand, revitalized and brought to spiritual life through the righteousness of Jesus, which by God's grace dwells exclusively in believers.

Third, though sin has brought about the state of death in our mortal bodies, yet if the Holy Spirit dwells in us, then our bodies will be given renewal of life, just as Jesus' dead body was renewed to eternal and immortal life at his resurrection. So it is that those of us who have the Holy Spirit actually dwelling in us, have our hope focused on the resurrection which will take place at the return of Christ. Nothing in this passage hints of our going to heaven at death. Rather it focuses our attention on the hope we have of our revivification at the second coming.

We must not be deceived. We must teach the unadulterated word of God and help his people to understand that only those who make the subjective choice to choose to receive God into their lives are the ones who can be indwelt by the Holy Spirit and subsequently become his adopted children who are granted salvation.

> John 1:12 – 13 But as many as received Him, to them He gave the right to become children of God, even to those who believe in His name, who were born, not of blood nor of the will of the flesh nor of the will of man, but of God.

GOD'S ENEMIES WILL BE CONVERTED

In Luke 13:22 – 30 we read the incident in which someone asks the Lord:

"Lord, are there just a few who are being saved?" One must note that Jesus does not indicate whether there will actually be few or many. However he does caution us to "strive to enter through the narrow door; for many, I tell you, will seek to enter and will not be able." Those who are excluded assume that he knows them because "We ate and drank in Your presence and You taught in our streets;".

In answering them, Jesus clarifies the course we ought to follow. He also relates the state of mind those who have not chosen Christ will have on that day (vs. 27 – 28).

> "He will say, 'I tell you, I do not know where you are from; Depart from Me, all you evildoers.' In that place there will be weeping and gnashing of teeth when you see Abraham and Isaac and Jacob and all the prophets in the kingdom of God, but yourselves being thrown out."

In this passage, Jesus is quoting from Psalm 6:8. In this psalm, the Holy Spirit inspired David to write of what would happen to his enemies, by extension, the enemies of Jesus, on the day of judgment.

> Psalm 6:8 – 10 Depart from me, all you who do iniquity, for the Lord has heard the voice of my weeping. The Lord has heard my supplication, the Lord receives my prayer. All my enemies will be ashamed and greatly dismayed; they shall turn back, they will suddenly be ashamed.

It is important to note here that the end result of those who are David's enemies is that they "will be ashamed and greatly dismayed; they shall turn back, they will suddenly be ashamed." David is describing the repentance and conversion that will occur to his enemies in the end. The two words used in this passage "turn back" indicate that they will indeed come to a state of repentance.

Gesenius notes the Hebrew word used here for "turn back" as *shuwb* (Strong's #7725) and defines it as: "to be converted as a sinner."[185]

Adam Clarke defines this statement as: "'May they be suddenly converted.' The original will bear this meaning and it is the most congenial to Christian principles."[186]

David looked forward to the day when his enemies, who maligned him mercilessly, would finally come to a state of their own personal shame and repentance.

With that clear implication in this psalm, which Jesus quotes regarding the coming judgment associated with the kingdom of God, why would he also overlook the implications of repentance in the psalm of those who have been rejected from the divine feast of Luke 13?

---

[185] H.W.F. Gesenius, *Gesenius' Hebrew-Chaldee Lexicon To The Old Testament*. (Grand Rapids, Baker Book House, 1984), 807.
[186] Adam Clarke, *Clarke's Commentary, Job – Malachi*. (Nashville, Abingdon Press, First released in England in 1810 and first published in the United States in 1824 by Abraham Paul for the New York branch of The Methodist Book Concern, no other dating given), 233.

In Psalm 6, the end of the enemies of David is that they finally come to repentance. He has no mention of them being cast into outer darkness and eternal suffering. It seems plausible that Jesus is using this quotation to bring his persecutors to their senses. To hear the line from David's psalm, "Depart from me, all you who do iniquity" would have been both shocking to the religious leaders of his day, as it should also be to us today, and an attention getting device designed to focus our minds on David's associated call to repentance.

Like David in his day, so will Jesus, in the eschatonal kingdom age, call those who were not raised in the first resurrection, to real repentance and confession of their sins in a last and merciful attempt to bring them to salvation. If David's enemies in his life will be called to personal shame and repentance in the age to come, why is it seemingly unrealistic and impossible to bring those, who ignorantly maligned Jesus in this life, to salvation in the next age? Scripture denotes the fact that those who were the enemies of the Lord in this life will finally come to repentance and acknowledgement of their personal shame and sin, in the judgment following the general resurrection of the millennial age.

> Revelation 1:7 Behold, He is coming with the clouds, and every eye will see Him, even those who pierced Him; and all the tribes of the earth will mourn over Him. So it is to be. Amen.

The Greek word translated "mourn" in this passage is *kapto*, and it means *to beat the breast in grief, cut down, lament, mourn, wail, bewail*.[187] This mourning is certainly of a repentant nature. If those who opposed Jesus come to repentance in the life of their resurrection, will not God honor that repentance and accept them as his adopted children as he does ourselves?

If the Lord deliberately offers the opportunity for repentance in the resurrection of nonbelievers to the enemies of David, then he must be serious about offering the possibility of eternal life even to the rest of mankind in that yet future timeframe. The Lord is not a respecter of persons, does nothing in vain and that certainly includes the granting of a time of genuine opportunity and days for salvation. This opportunity is given to all who have not yet had a real time of salvation.

A great purpose of the Lord is to bring those who hate him to salvation. Since we human beings are so dull of mind, stiff-necked and hard-headed to work with, we often need to be shocked into repentance and the admission of our sinful nature. That is what Jesus sought to accomplish in Luke

---

[187] James Strong, *Strong's Exhaustive Concordance of the Bible, Updated Edition.* (Peabody, Hendrickson Publishers, Inc., 2007), 1642.

13:27. In the general judgment before the throne of God, many will come to salvation on that day when they are finally and publicly exposed to be the vile sinners that they really are. That day, from the perspective of this current life, seemed to be only a fable and so far off that they never gave it much thought. Nevertheless, the day will come, and they will be greatly surprised and equally ashamed of themselves and their publicly exposed sins. They had lived lives of license and permissiveness only to be finally caught unawares on that great day of judgment that is yet to come.

> Ecclesiastes 8:11 Because the sentence against an evil deed is not executed quickly, therefore the hearts of the sons of men among them are given fully to do evil.

PUBLIC SHAMING

The Lord will utilize the tool of public shaming to both stun and convince sinners that they really do have something to repent of. On that day the judgment of the wicked will be very public and extremely humiliating for all who are subject to it. As any good parent, in what pop psychologists refer to as "tough love", God will use the tools of shame and guilt to reach his children and will give them every opportunity and help in their coming to a state of genuine and deep repentance.

Packer recognizes that the judgment will be humbling for all people. He emphasizes that it is best to come to God, now in this life, rather than face his scrutiny then.

> Paul refers to the fact that we must all appear before Christ's judgment seat as "the terror of the Lord" (2 Cor. 5:11 KJV), and well he might. Jesus the Lord, like his Father, is holy and pure; we are neither. We live under his eye, he knows our secrets, and on judgment day the whole of our past life will be played back, as it were, before him, and brought under review. If we know ourselves at all, we know we are not fit to face him. What then are we to do? The New Testament answer is: *Call on the coming Judge to be your present Savior.* As Judge, he is the law, but as Savior he is the gospel. Run from him now, and you will meet him as Judge then – and without hope. Seek him now, and you will find him (for "he that seeketh findeth"), and you will then discover that you are looking forward to that future meeting with joy, knowing that there is now "no condemnation for those who are in Christ Jesus" (Rom. 8:1).[188]

---

[188] J.I. Packer, *Knowing God.* (Downers Grove, InterVarsity Press, 1993), 146 – 147.

Imagine the Lord, on the day of judgment, mimicking a popular late-night comedian, saying, "We have the video!" Imagine the effect of exposing the sins of unbelievers, "and on judgment day the whole of our past life will be played back, as it were, before him, and brought under review." No doubt, for the first time in their lives the unrepentant will finally understand that they do have sin to repent of, and that they desperately need to beg the forgiveness of their Redeemer. Not until they come to a state of deep humility can God begin to work with them in bringing them to salvation. On that day of the public revealing and exposure of their sins, and in their intensity of shame and personal humiliation, most people will finally be open to repentance and confession of their sins in an effort to receive the salvation that the Lord has always been so willing to grant them. Scripture makes it evident that ultimately all people will bow in submission before the Lord of Glory.

> Philippians 2:9 – 11 For this reason also, God highly exalted Him, and bestowed on Him the name which is above every name, so that at the name of Jesus every knee will bow of those who are in heaven and on earth and under the earth, and that every tongue will confess that Jesus Christ is Lord, to the glory of God the Father.

I am not blind to the fact that many Christians do not agree with this theological position. Ever since the late 19th century, in which Christian theology acquired a concentration on German Rationalism and its associated infection of the church with the rejection of any teaching on divine wrath and judgment, we have been held hostage to an inaccurate view of God. As a result we have today what Packer labels *Santa Claus theology* in which God is a great gift giver and is only perceived as a "good guy" who will not send anyone to hell or judge anyone in anyway that they would consider to be harsh.

> But on the basis of the Santa Claus theology, sins create no problem, and atonement becomes needless; God's active favor extends no less to those who disregard his commands than to those who keep them. The idea that God's attitude to me is affected by whether or not I do what he says has no place in the thought of the man on the street, and any attempt to show the need for fear in God's presence, for trembling at his word, gets written off as impossibly old fashioned – "Victorian," "Puritan" and "sub-Christian."[189]

At the coming day of judgment, the grace of God will be magnificently manifest to all as the Lord pardons everyone who requests it in true humility.

---

[189] *J.I. Packer, Knowing God. (Downer's Grove, InterVarsity Press, 1993), 160.*

In his grace salvation will be offered to all. Salvation will be willingly granted by the Lord. But for most, that salvation will not be accomplished until they have been humbled and they finally come to genuine repentance. In the process of coming to salvation, repentance is absolutely essential. Scripture reveals that repentance leads to salvation and that without repentance there can be no salvation.

>2 Corinthians 7:10 For the sorrow that is according to the will of God produces a repentance without regret, leading to salvation, but the sorrow of the world produces death.

In God's grace, his tough love plan is exhibited to make salvation possible to all mankind. Everyone who has ever lived will have opportunity at the eschatonal judgment if they had not had the full opportunity already afforded to them in this age.

>Titus 2:11 For the grace of God has appeared, bringing salvation to all men.

CHAPTER NINE
CONCLUSION

Chapter Nine

Conclusion

*Rather than wallpaper over these holes and renovate our theology
in a vain attempt to mask or repair problems,
perhaps it's time we considered bulldozing the house and starting over,
laying a new foundation in Christ our blessed hope.[190]*

As a result of this study it has become apparent that traditional Christianity's theological teaching on the matter of salvation and punishment leaves much to be desired. In fact, if the findings of this treatise are true and if they were incorporated into mainstream Christian doctrine and practice, then our whole perspective on the subject of salvation and damnation would be dramatically changed. In effect the whole house of cards of our historic dogma would come tumbling down. Not only would our views on salvation change, but equally important, our views on the judgment of God and the punishment of those who refuse him would also be substantially altered.

Imagine the day when Christian pastors and teachers would no longer use the threat of ever-burning in hell fire and never ending suffering in excruciating pain for those who refused the way of Christ. Even for those innocents who never even heard of him, much less the true gospel of salvation. No longer would hell be used as a goad or as a whip to keep people in line and submissive to intolerant leadership.

Rather than focusing on eternal pain, which is not biblical, we could focus on exhibiting the very mercy and grace of God through our own example and teaching. We could focus on promoting the good news of the kingdom of God and the eternal possibilities for us as we serve the Lord as sub-kings and priests over his flock. We would be guided by the example of his beneficent rule. We could teach of the eternity that faces us in terms of how much we could discover and learn of the mind of God, and how wonderful it would be to be forever mining the depths of the mind of the omniscient God of all the universe. That eternity in which we would participate with him in the development of the promise given through the prophet Isaiah in 9:7, that "there will be no end to the increase of his government or of peace."

We could teach the biblical truth that there will be no more tears of sorrow, no more death, no mourning, no crying or pain. That being true

---

[190] Bradley Jersak, *Her Gates Will Never Be Shut.* (Eugene, WIPF & Stock, 2009), 188 – 189.

because the lake of fire will long since have ceased its work of consuming the wicked in a relatively short period of time.

Hopefully the reader has noticed that the points and arguments that I make in this book are not founded in emotion. Rather the raw black and white truth of Scripture has been my evidence and defense. It is my experience that the arguments emoting from the defenders of Christian traditional teachings are too often themselves based on emotion with a desire to defend the bulwarks of tradition against the hard fact of scriptural research. This volume and its conclusions are based on what Scripture and historical fact actually say rather than on my own wishful thinking.

The major findings evident in the research and compilation of scriptural truth in this book have led to the following conclusions, chapter by chapter:

Chapter One: God makes complete provision for every individual to have an adequate time of spiritual education and a moment of decision regarding the choice to either accept or reject salvation in Jesus Christ. That opportunity may come in this lifetime or at the general judgment in the eschatonal age.

Chapter Two: God overlooks our spiritual ignorance and does not judge us for what we do not understand.

Chapter Three: The biblical soul is the temporary and mortal life of this current day. The soul is not metaphysical as taught in ancient Greek philosophy and consequently is not immortal at this moment.

Chapter Four: The Lord will not consign anyone to the flames of the Lake of Fire without first giving them full education regarding the gospel offer of salvation.

Chapter Five: Knowledge of the future coming resurrection is what gave hope to ancient Israel. They saw the resurrection and revivification of mankind to take place on this earth.

Chapter Six: Jesus' clear teaching in the gospels is that the dead are "asleep." The first-century church understood that the dead are asleep until the second coming of the Lord.

Chapter Seven: Unquenchable fire is unquenchable only as long as God keeps it ignited. "The Lord our God is a consuming fire."

Chapter Eight: God does not punish for ignorance. Even his enemies will be brought to a state of repentance.

Chapter Nine: Platonic dualism should not be the basis for Christian Theology. Rather, we need to return fully to the authority of divinely inspired Scripture, the Bible.

In this book, I conclude that God is not a sadistic monster who delights in willfully punishing the unbelieving for an eternity of excruciating pain for multiplied billions of years without end. According to traditional Christian teaching, that punishment is to be inflicted upon the hopelessly wicked, though their crime of rejection of God lasts perhaps for only a short few days or years. In spite of their own ignorance in not even knowing the Lord, never having had real opportunity to know the gospel, our faulty theology consigns them to eternal suffering as immortal beings in inextinguishable flames. That, in my opinion, is an absolutely wrong perspective. I also conclude that the saved will find no delight whatsoever in the suffering of unbelievers.

God would not grant us immortality as his faithful servants forever if he were unsure about our state of fidelity to him. Every time we fall on our knees in repentance before the throne of the judge of all mankind, he is deciding our case in our favor in this life, in the here and now.

In the Gospel of John, Jesus assures us of this very fact.
> John 5:24 Truly, truly, I say to you, he who hears My word, and believes Him who sent Me, has eternal life, and does not come into judgment, but has passed out of death into life.

The writer of the book of Hebrews also assures us that at the second coming, the Lord will not come to judge the sins of believers. We notice that our case will already have been decided and as the forgiven and redeemed we will face no additional judgment of condemnation. When he comes to us it will be "without reference to sin."
> Hebrews 9:28 So Christ also, having been offered once to bear the sins of many, will appear a second time for salvation without reference to sin, to those who eagerly await Him.

The marvelous truth of this study is that God loves us all. He determined that in this life he would accept many, but not all, to serve him in his eternal administration. Most of the remainder of mankind will actually be granted salvation opportunity in the general resurrection in the eschatological end of the age. You and I have the opportunity to accept his call now and serve in his administration forever as glorified spirit beings of unbelievable ability and authority under Christ.

I challenge us all to proclaim that good news from the rooftops instead of trying to sell fire insurance. Yes, God's wrath is real and will some day be on full display as he eliminates the wicked. Yes, we need to respect his power to judge and to convict, but we also need to understand his grace and mercy, the fact that he will not hold us accountable for what we do not understand. We need to understand and proclaim that if not in this life, then in the next, God will make abundant opportunity available, to all who rise in the second resurrection, for learning his plan and his gospel message of life and blessing. There is great hope for all mankind and I want to be a part of the solution to the problem of sin and evil. That solution is based on God's eternal love for his children, rather than trying to coercively scare them into a relationship with the Lord. A relationship built on love is what God desires, not a relationship of terror and unmerited fear of him as a sadistic torturer.

Is this message of God's love one that you want to be part of and to proclaim and have inclusion in? Then please join me in this greatest revelation of the love of God ever known.

I believe that because of the gracious unmerited pardon of the Lord, the day is coming when absolutely every knee of every person who ever lived will, in all humility, bow before him in the acknowledgement that Jesus is Lord, he is Sovereign, he is in charge, he is our all-merciful and loving God!

> Philippians 2:9-11 For this reason also, God highly exalted Him, and bestowed on Him the name which is above every name, so that at the name of Jesus every knee will bow of those who are in heaven and on earth and under the earth, and that every tongue will confess that Jesus Christ is Lord, to the glory of God the Father.

BIBLIOGRAPHY

Albrecht, Greg, *Does God Send People To Hell Because Of Their Ignorance?* Plain Truth Ministries, Oct. 25, 2010, PTE E-Update. www.ptm.org/uni/resources/ptmupdate/102510/l.html.

Anderson, Ray S., *Theology, Death and Dying.* Worcester, Billing and Sons Ltd., 1986.

Audi, Robert, General Editor. *The Cambridge Dictionary of Philosophy, Second Edition*, Cambridge, Cambridge University Press, 1999.

Augustine, Saint, *City of God.* Translated by Henry Bettenson. London, Penguin Books Group, 2003.

Augustine, Saint, *Confessions.* Translated by R.S. Pinecoffin. London, Penguin Books Group, 1961.

Baker, Sharon L., *Razing Hell.* Louisville, Westminster John Knox Press, 2010.

Ball, Bryan W., *The Soul Sleepers, Christian Mortalism from Wycliffe to Priestley*, Cambridge, James Clarke & Co., 2008.

Bauer, Walter, *A Greek-English Lexicon Of The New Testament And Other Early Christian Literature, Third Edition.* Ed. Danker, Frederick William. Chicago, University of Chicago Press, 2000.

Beale, Gregory K., Block, Daniel I., Ferguson, Sinclair B., Mohler, R. Albert Jr., Moo, Douglas J., Morgan, Christopher W., Packer, J.I., Peterson, Robert A., Yarbrough, Robert W., *Hell Under Fire.* Grand Rapids, Zondervan Publishing Co., 2004.

Beasley – Murray, George R., *John, Second Edition*, Word Biblical Commentary. Nashville, Thomas Nelson Publishers, 1999.

Bell, Rob, *Love Wins, A Book About Heaven, Hell, And The Fate Of Every Person Who Ever Lived.* New York, Harper One, 2011.

Broderick, Robert C., *The Catholic Encyclopedia.* Nashville, Thomas Nelson Inc., Publishers, 1976.

Brown, Francis, D.D., D. Litt., Driver, S.R., D.D., Litt.D. and Briggs, Charles, D.D., D. Litt., *The Brown-Driver-Briggs Hebrew and English Lexicon.* Peabody, Hendrickson Publishers, Inc., 2005.

Burns, Norman T., *Christian Mortalism from Tyndale to Milton.* Cambridge, Harvard University Press, 1972.

Calvin, John, *Institutes of the Christian Religion.* Translated by Henry Beveridge. Peabody, Hendrickson Publishers, 2008.

Clarke, Adam, *Clarke's Commentary, Job – Malachi.* USA, Abingdon Press, 1977.

Clarke, Adam, *Clarke's Commentary, Matthew – Revelation.* USA, Abingdon Press, 1977.

Cohen, Shaye J.D., *From the Maccabees to the Mishna.* Philadelphia, The Westminster Press, 1987.

Crockett, William V., General Editor, *Four Views on Hell.* Grand Rapids, Zondervan Publishing, 1996.

Cullmann, Oscar, *Immortality of the Soul or Resurrection of the Dead?* London, The Epworth Press, 1958.

Danker, Frederick William, General Editor, Walter Bauer's *A Greek-EnglishLexicon of the New Testament and Other Early Christian Literature, Third Edition*. Chicago. The University of Chicago Press, 2004.

Edwards, David L.; Stott, John, *Evangelical Essentials*. Downers Grove, Intervarsity Press, 1989.

Elwell, Walter A., General Editor. *Evangelical Dictionary of Theology*. Grand Rapids, Baker Books, 1997.

Feazell, Michael, *Lazarus and the Rich Man: A Tale of Unbelief*. Christian Odyssey, February – March, 2011.

Feinberg, John S., *The Many Faces of Evil*. Wheaton, Crossway Books, 2004.

Fox, John, *Fox's Book of Martyrs*. Forbush, William Byron, D.D., Editor. Grand Rapids, Zondervan Publishing House, 1978.

Froom, Le Roy Edwin, *The Conditionalist Faith Of Our Fathers, Volume II*. Washington, D.C., Review and Herald Publishing Association. 1965.

Fudge, Edward William, *The Fire That Consumes*. Bletchley, UK., Paternoster Press, 2005.

Fudge, Edward William and Peterson, Robert A., *Two Views of Hell*. Downers Grove, InterVarsity Press, 2000.

Gaston, Lloyd, *The Romans Debate*. Editor, Donfried, Karl P. Peabody, Hendrickson Publishing, 1991.

Geisler, Norman Dr., *Systematic Theology, Volume Three*. Minneapolis, Bethany House, 2004.

Gesenius, H.W.F., *Gesenius' Hebrew-Chaldee Lexicon To The Old Testament*. Grand Rapids, Baker Book House, 1984.

Grace Communion International, *Statement of Beliefs*. Glendora, CA.,2009.

Green, Michael, *Evangelism Through The Local Church*. Nashville, Thomas Nelson Publishers, 1992.

Guthrie, Donald, *New Testament Theology*. Downers Grove, InterVarsity Press, 1981.

Hamilton, Victor P., *The Book of Genesis Chapters 1 – 17*. Grand Rapids, William B. Eerdmans Publishing Company, 1990.

Harris, Richard Laird; Archer, Gleason L. Jr. and Waltke, Bruce K., *Theological Wordbook of the Old Testament*. Chicago, Moody Press, 1980.

Hodge, Charles, *Systematic Theology, Volume III*. Peabody, HendricksonPublishers, 2003.

House, Paul R., *Old Testament Theology*. Downers Grove, Intervarsity Press, 1998.

Hoekema, Anthony A., *The Bible and the Future*. Grand Rapids, William B.Eerdmans Publishing Co., 1994.

Jersak, Bradley, *Her Gates Will Never Be Shut*. Eugene, WIPF & Stock,2009.

Johnson, Alan F., *Revelation, Volume 12, The Expositor's Bible Commentary*. General Editor Frank E. Gaebelein. Grand Rapids, Zondervan Publishing House, 1999.

Kaiser, Walter C., Jr., *Toward an Old Testament Theology*. Grand Rapids, Zondervan Publishing House, 1991.

Kaufmann, Yehezkel, *Great Ages and Ideas of the Jewish People*. Edited by Leo W. Schwartz. New York, The Modern Library, 1956.

Keil, C.F. and Delitzsch F., *Keil and Delitzsch Commentary On The Old Testament, Volume* One. Peabody, Hendrickson Publishers, 1989.

Keil, C.F. and Delitzsch F., *Keil and Delitzsch Commentary On The Old Testament, Volume Three*. Peabody, Hendrickson Publishers, 1989.

Ladd, George Eldon, *A Theology of the New Testament*. Grand Rapids, William B. Eerdmans Publishing Co., 1993.

Ladd, George Eldon, *The Pattern of New Testament Truth*. Grand Rapids, William B. Eerdmans Publishing Co., 1968.

Levenson, Jon D. *Resurrection And The Restoration Of Israel*. New Haven, Yale University Press, 2006.

Liefeld, Walter L., *Luke, from The Expositor's Commentary, Volume 8*. General Editor, Gabelein, Frank E. Grand Rapids, Zondervan Publishing House, 1984.

Lockman Foundation, *New American Standard Bible*. Anaheim, Foundation Publications, Inc., 1995.

Martin, Ralph P., *2 Corinthians*. Nashville, Thomas Nelson Publishers, 1986.

Matthews, Kenneth A., *Genesis 11:27 – 50:26*. General Editor, E. Ray Clendenen. Nashville, Broadman & Holmen Publishers, 2006.

Milton, John, *Paradise Regained*, (1671).

Murphy, Roland, *Ecclesiastes*. Dallas, Word Books, 1992.

Odom, Robert Leo, *Is Your Soul Immortal?* Ukiah, CA., Orion Publishing, 2007.

Olson, Roger E., *Arminian Theology*. Downers Grove, IVP Academic, 2006.

Ormerod, Neil, *Creation, Grace, and Redemption*. Maryknoll, NY., Orbis Books, 2007.

Oswalt, John N., *The Book of Isaiah, Chapters 1 – 39*. Edited by R.K. Harrison. Grand Rapids, William B. Eerdmans Publishing Co., 1986.

Packer, J.I., *Knowing God*. Downer's Grove, InterVarsity Press, 1993.

Parker, J., Editor, *The First Prayer-Book...of King Edward VI [1549]*. Oxford and London, 1883.

Pieper, Josef, *Death and Immortality*. South Bend, St. Augustine's Press, 2000.

Payne, J. Burton, *The Wycliffe Bible Commentary*. Charles F. Pfeiffer, Editor. Chicago, Moody Press, 1977.

Pinnock, Clark H., *Four Views of Hell, from Chapter Four, The Conditional View*. General Editor, Crockett, William. Grand Rapids, Zondervan Publishing, 1996.

Pinnock, Clark H., *The Grace of God and the Will of Man.* Minneapolis, Bethany House Publishers, 1995.

Plass, Ewald M., Compiler. *What Luther Says.* St. Louis, Concordia Publishing House, 1959.

Powys, David, *'Hell': A Hard Look at a Hard Question.* Bletchley, UK.,Paternoster Press, 1997.

Rodgers, Thomas R., D. Min., *The Panorama Of The Old Testament.* Newburgh, Trinity Press, 2003.

Ryrie, Charles Caldwell, Th.D., Ph.D., *Ryrie Study Bible, Expanded Edition.* Chicago, Moody Press, 1995.

Salmond, Stewart Dingwall Fordyce, *The Christian Doctrine of Immortality.* Danvers, General Books LLC., 2009

Sanders, John, Editor, *What About Those Who Have Never Heard*? Downers Grove, InterVarsity Press, 1995.

Selwyn, E.G., *The First Epistle of St. Peter.* London, Macmillan, 1961.

Skevington, A. Wood, *Ephesians, from The Expositor's Bible Commentary, Volume 11.* General Editor, Frank E. Gaebelein. Grand Rapids, Zondervan Publishing House, 1984.

Stein, Robert H., *Luke, From The New American Commentary, Volume 24.* General Editor, David S. Dockery. Nashville, Broadman Press, 1992.

Strong, James, *Enhanced Strong's Lexicon.* Woodside Bible Fellowship, 1996. From Libronix Digital Library System, copyright 2004.

Strong, James, Strong's *Exhaustive Concordance of the Bible, UpdatedEdition.* Peabody, Hendrickson Publishers, Inc., 2007.

Thayer, Joseph H., *Thayer's Greek-English Lexicon of the New Testament.* Grand Rapids, Baker Book House, 1977.

Thielman, Frank, *Theology of the New Testament.* Grand Rapids, Zondervan, 2005.

Torrance, Thomas F., *The Christian Frame Of Mind.* Colorado Springs, Helmers & Howard, 1989.

Unger, Merrill F., *Unger's Bible Dictionary.* Chicago, Moody Press, 1979.

VanGemeren, Willem A., *Interpreting the Prophetic Word.* Grand Rapids, Zondervan Publishing House, 1990.

Von Balthasar, Hans Urs, *Dare We Hope "That All Men Be Saved"?.* San Francisco, Ignatius Press, 1988.

Walvoord, John F., Hayes, Zachary J. and Pinnock, Clark H., *Four Views on Hell.* General Editor, Crockett, William V. Grand Rapids, Zondervan Publishing Co., 1996.

Warfield, Benjamin Breckinridge, D.D., LL.D., *The Works of Benjamin B. Warfield, Volume IX, Studies in Theology.* New York, Oxford University Press, Inc., 2003.

Wenham, David, *The Parables of Jesus.* Downers Grove, InterVarsity Press, 1989.

Wenham, Gordon J., *Genesis 1 – 15.* Waco, Word Books, Publisher, 1987.

Wenham, John W., *The Goodness of God*. London, InterVarsity Press, 1974.

Whiston, William, *Josephus Complete Works*. Grand Rapids, Kregel Publications, 1969.

Wink, Walter, *The Human Being*. Minneapolis, Fortress Press, 2002.

Wood, A. Skevington, *Ephesians, From The Expositor's Bible Commentary, Volume 11*. General Editor, Gabelein, Frank E. Grand Rapids, Zondervan Publishing House, 1984.

Wright, N.T., *The Resurrection Of The Son Of God*, Minneapolis, Fortress Press, 2003.

Wright, N.T., *Surprised By Hope*. New York, Harper Collins, 2008.

Yarbrough, Robert W., *Hell Under Fire, Chapter Three*. General Editors, Morgan, Christopher W. and Peterson, Robert A. Grand Rapids, Zondervan Publishing, 2004.

Yonge, C.D., trans., *The Works of Philo*. Peabody, Hendrickson Publishers, 1993.

CPSIA information can be obtained at www.ICGtesting.com
Printed in the USA
LVOW040114090212

267844LV00002B/3/P